FROM INSTITUTIONS TO INDEPENDENCE

A History of People with Disabilities
in Northwest Ohio

Barbara L. Floyd, Editor

The University of Toledo Press
Toledo, Ohio
2010

Copyright 2010
by
The University of Toledo Press
utoledopress.com

All rights reserved
Manufactured in the United States of America

From Institutions to Independence
A History of People with Disabilities
in Northwest Ohio

The publication of this book was supported in part by donations
from the following organizations:

The Ability Center of Greater Toledo

and

Lott Industries

Book design by Joan Bishop, The University of Toledo
Project assistance by Tricia Salata

Thomas Barden, Joel Lipman, Molly Schiever, editors

Library of Congress Control Number: 2010938137

ISBN: 978-0-932259-07-3

Dedication

This book is dedicated to the memory of Alva Bunker, whose personal story inspired an international movement to help children with disabilities that continues today.

It is also dedicated to the thousands of other people with disabilities, like Alva, who have been a part of our history but whose lives have been forgotten.

Table of Contents

Acknowledgements iii

Preface—Jim Ferris iv

Introduction—Barbara L. Floyd vi

1. **Attics, Almshouses, and Asylums:** 1
   Care for People with Mental Illness
   —*Kimberly Brownlee*

2. **Sheltered Workshops and Social Clubs:** 21
   Services for Vision and Hearing Impaired Persons
   —*Jennifer Free*

3. **Society and the "Cripple":** From Seclusion to Education 41
   —*Barbara L. Floyd*

4. **Creating the "Perfect" Human:** Eugenics and 59
   Disabled People
   —*Tamara Jones*

5. **The Disabling Disease:** Polio 73
   —*Barbara L. Floyd*

6. **Custodial Institutions to Community Care:** 93
   Assisting Developmentally Disabled People
   —*David G. Chelminski*

7. **"Hire the Handicapped":** Vocational Rehabilitation 113
   for Disabled Persons
   —*Barbara L. Floyd*

8. **Overcoming Obstacles:** From Deinstitutionalization 129
   to Independent Living
   —*Barbara L. Floyd and Tamara Jones*

9. **Who Fits the Label of "Disabled?":** 149
   The Historical Meaning of Disability
   —*Barbara L. Floyd*

About the Authors 156

Appendix

1. **From Institutions to Independence:** A Timeline 157
   of Disability Laws and Regulations
   —*Jennifer Free*

2. **Disability Terminology Timeline** 162
   —*Kimberly Brownlee*

Primary Sources, Ward M. Canaday Center 163

Selected Bibliography 164

Index 165

Acknowledgements

There are many people to thank for making this book possible. First and foremost are my coauthors: Kimberly Brownlee, Tamara Jones, Jennifer Free, and David Chelminski. Also, my sincere thanks to the Ability Center of Greater Toledo for helping to underwrite the cost of its production, and the University of Toledo Press for recognizing the importance of this topic to the fabric of our community and thereby agreeing to publish it. Also, to Joan Bishop for the volume's beautiful design. My thanks to all of these people—this is really their work.

An advisory board provided valuable insight into a topic that we frankly knew little about when we began our research. Those people include Diane Britton, Chris Diefenthaler, Michael Mechlowitz, Shelley Papenfuse, Christine Raber, Liz Sheets, Jerry Van Hoy, Jane Weber, Wendy Wiitala, Dan Wilkins, and Sharon Yaros. Jim Ferris also read the catalog that accompanied the original exhibit and made valuable suggestions. My thanks to them, and especially to Jim Ferris for providing the preface to this book.

Several organizations and individuals loaned us material for the original exhibit, some of which is included in the photographs in this book. It is a much more riveting and informative volume because of the photos. My thanks to the Center for Archival Collections at Bowling Green State University; Northcoast Behavioral Healthcare; Sharon Yaros; the Lucas County Board of Developmental Disabilities; the Local History and Genealogy Department of the Toledo-Lucas County Public Library; Gendron, Inc.; Goodwill Industries of Northwest Ohio, Inc.; the Wood County Board of Developmental Disabilities; the Wood County Historical Society; and the Museum of disABILITY History. Unless otherwise noted, the photographs in this book are from the collections of the Ward M. Canaday Center.

Barbara L. Floyd, editor
November 2010

Preface
By Jim Ferris
Director, University of Toledo Disability Studies Program
and Ability Center of Greater Toledo Endowed Chair

Disability has been a part of human experience as long as there have been humans. But as historians are only recently coming to realize, this crucial aspect of the human story has been ignored in written histories. As historian Douglas Baynton observed, "Disability is everywhere in history, once you begin looking for it, but conspicuously absent in the histories we write."

From Institutions to Independence: A History of People with Disabilities in Northwest Ohio is an important step toward redressing that conspicuous absence. The Regional Disability History Archive Project at the Ward M. Canaday Center for Special Collections has begun the vital work of collecting materials that document disability history. This book details the richness of that work.

Why is it important to place disabled people* in history—in the histories that we write? Certainly it is important to document that disabled people make contributions too; countering the long-running canard that disabled people are worthless can hardly be overvalued. But recognizing the role of disability in human history is necessary for an even more important reason: disabled people are and always have been an essential part of the human fabric, and we ignore that fact at our own peril.

Why peril? It is dangerous for humankind not to see the world as it is—especially when we think we are seeing it clearly, especially when we are using that flawed perspective on the world to take actions that affect the lives of real people. How we think about the world and how we understand our places within it have great consequences. When we act as if disabled people are only "consumers," are only what the Nazis called "useless eaters," we lose sight of the truth that our tribe, our nation, is not made up of the independent here and the dependent over there, that we are all in fact interdependent, all part of a grand fabric of which none of us is able to step outside, that none of us can step back far enough to see fully, even though we might like to think we can see it pretty well.

What makes up this fabric? The ideas and institutions, the patterns and textures, are certainly important. But there is no fabric without the individual threads—no one of them dictates the whole, but each is essential to it. When we decide to ignore a significant portion of the fabric, it diminishes our perspective on and understanding of the whole.

Without disabled people, there is no true, accurate picture of human history—of the world, of the nation, of northwest Ohio. Strong archives flesh out our understanding by providing details. This archive, as detailed in this book, is particularly strong at this point in providing contemporaneous information about how those who sought to improve the lives of disabled people set about their work and how they understood what they were doing. This is far from the end of the story, of course, but it is an important step in telling this vital and overlooked story. And the book heralds an important educational resource for those who study disability and disabled lives through history.

In profoundly important ways, the world is the way it is due to the decisions men and women made in the past. And we cannot understand our world as it is without some understanding of how we got here. This book, and the archive it heralds, are important pieces we can use to build, to deepen our understanding.

Some day, others will write histories of today. They will look at this time and place, seeing what their ideas and the historical record of artifacts and texts allows them to see. Will they see the disabled people of today? Where will they see them? This book, and this archive, suggest that disabled people will not be hidden away, will not be overlooked, as was past practice. By collecting these materials, by caring for them and making them available to both the scholars and the public, by insisting on our past, we articulate a present, and we claim a future. Ultimately, that is what the Regional Disability History Archive Project offers us: the possibility of a future of greater understanding. This is an important way of keeping faith with those who came before; this is part of fulfilling our responsibility to those who will follow us. Here is where we came from; let us learn from it as we seek to build that better future.

* I use the phrase "disabled people" instead of the people-first phrase "people with disabilities" in keeping with the call from Simi Linton and others to center disabled experience and claim a political identity. See *Claiming Disability: Knowledge and Identity* by Simi Linton (New York: NYU Press, 1998).

INTRODUCTION
By Barbara L. Floyd

To seek out and archive "real" disability history will provide a body of knowledge that will forever give substance and credibility to the thoughts, dreams, and actions of those who went before.

—Disabled Toledoan Dan Wilkins,
on the significance of the Ward M. Canaday Center's
Regional Disability History Archive Project

The genesis for *From Institutions to Independence* was a 2008 exhibition by the same name in the Ward M. Canaday Center for Special Collections. The exhibition—and this book—examine an aspect of our community's history that has been largely unknown and untold. The reason for our ignorance and neglect of disability history is undoubtedly because society has long devalued those who are disabled. Persons with disabilities not only look and act differently, in sometimes unpleasant ways, but they are reminders of the fragility of life—that any of us could find ourselves disabled at any time due to accident, illness, or age. Throughout much of our history, we have preferred that disabled persons be locked away and their lives (and history) lived out of our sight.

But why is this history important for us to know? Because history binds us together, creates an identity as a community, and helps us to understand where we fit within society. It validates our experiences and gives a greater meaning to our daily existence. While historians during the past thirty years have worked to document the historical experience of many underrepresented groups for these reasons, disabled people have been largely excluded from efforts to be more inclusive.

But historians do not bear the entire blame for this void in our historical consciousness. Archivists, too, are at fault. The records that archivists choose to collect shape our historical knowledge in significant ways. Prior to the 1960s, the archival profession collected records that reflected history as the story of the privileged few. Beginning with the new social history of the 1960s, archivists branched out and collected records of underrepresented groups such as labor unions, women, and minorities. Yet to this day, people with disabilities have been largely neglected in these attempts to more completely document our nation's past.

In 2001, the University of Toledo Ward M. Canaday Center began to address this void in its collections. That year, the Ability Center of Greater Toledo, a center for independent living whose own history dates back to 1920, donated $1.9 million to create the Disability Studies Program at UT. Using a humanities-based perspective rather than a medical-scientific one, the academic program emphasizes disability as a cultural category of analysis. As part of this initiative, the Canaday Center, working with the program's interim director Dr. Patricia Murphy, sought to collect historical records that would serve as a research collection available to students and faculty in Disability Studies and related fields. After the Center began to collect these materials, we discovered that barely a handful of archival repositories in the nation have disability history as a major focus of archival collecting. Because of the uniqueness of what became known as the Regional Disability History Archive Project, the Center has attracted not only records documenting disability in northwest Ohio, but also several collections of national significance. Of particular note in the latter category are the papers of the late Hugh Gregory Gallagher, one of the founders of the disability rights movement and a noted disability scholar.

With a core group of collections documenting disability history, the Canaday Center decided to mount a public exhibition that presented these materials in the first local examination of disability history. The exhibit was made possible by a Program for Academic Excellence grant from the UT Office of the Provost. The exhibit received the 2008 Community Access Award from the Ability Center of Greater Toledo; an Ohio Public Images award from the Public Images Network, an organization promoting positive perceptions of people with disabilities; and the Philip M. Hamer and Elizabeth Hamer Kegan Award for public awareness from the Society of American Archivists. In addition, Kimberly Brownlee and I received the Edith Rathbun Award for Community Outreach and Engagement from UT in 2009 for the Disability History Archive Project.

Like the exhibit, the book is arranged topically, but also follows a somewhat chronological path in documenting how society reacted to various disabilities and began to address persons affected. Subject areas are discussed within the national context, then at the local level, in chapters written by Canaday Center staff.

From Institutions to Independence begins with an examination of how our community has cared for those with mental illness. Chapter 1 relays how Toledo pioneered a new kind of mental health facility where patients lived in small, family-like dwellings rather than in large wards. This "cottage system" approach influenced how other state-supported mental health facilities were built in the early twentieth century. In its early years, the Toledo State Hospital focused on work, diversion, recreation, regimentation, and a degree of personal freedom as the best methods for helping its residents.

Chapter 2 examines programs for those with vision and hearing impairments, issues brought to the public's attention by Helen Keller in her 1903 autobiography, *The Story of My Life*. Keller was a powerful spokesperson for deaf and blind causes; her 1925 appearance locally had a lasting impact. After Keller's speech to the convention of Lions Clubs International, at Cedar Point in Sandusky, the Clubs took up blindness as the focus of their philanthropic efforts, still a major emphasis of their fundraising. The chapter also recounts the efforts of the Sight Center of Northwest Ohio.

Chapter 3 reveals the amazing but little-known story of how one young Toledo boy, born with severe deformities at the turn of the twentieth century, inspired an international movement to help children with disabilities. The story of Alva Bunker is one of quiet courage and the help given him by the Rotary Club of Toledo changed his life. Rotary International continues to change the lives of thousands today as it works to eradicate polio worldwide.

Chapter 4 deals with a social movement that sought not to help those with disabilities, but rather to eliminate them. Supporters of eugenics, the study and practice of selective breeding, believed the best way to improve society was to ensure those with disabilities would not have children themselves. Eugenics had the support of many social progressives in the early twentieth century, including Scott Nearing, dean of the UT College of Arts and Sciences from 1915-1917, and John Williams Jones, superintendent of the Ohio State School for the Deaf in 1917. Eugenics would see its ultimate application in Nazi Germany where those with disabilities were sterilized—and slaughtered.

Chapter 5 is the story of the impact of polio on our community and nation. Polio knew no class lines and could incapacitate a president as readily as a pauper. The race to discover a vaccine against polio became a national obsession funded by millions of dimes collected by mothers and schoolchildren. It made Dr. Jonas Salk a hero. But for those for whom the 1955 vaccine came too late, polio left a lifetime of struggle for strength and independence. In Toledo, the Toledo Rotary built a convalescent center for northwest Ohio children recovering from the disease that served as home, hospital, and school.

The activism of the Mother's March on Polio influenced parents of children with developmental disabilities in the 1950s to advocate for better care and educational opportunities.

Chapter 6 examines how parents in Lucas and Wood counties sought to create schools that would allow their children to live outside the custodial institutions where many were locked away. It tells the story of one Toledo woman who sought to teach developmentally disabled children and to create facilities where they could learn vocational skills to support themselves as adults. Today, Lott Industries—started by Josina Lott as the first noninstitutional program in the nation to provide vocational training for developmentally disabled people—serves over 1,200 people each day.

Chapter 7 examines the "Hire the Handicapped" movement of the postwar years. This program, funded by the federal government to encourage employment of disabled World War II veterans, was the beginning of the movement by disabled people to gain independence. In Toledo, organizations such as Goodwill Industries and the Conlon Center worked to remove barriers to employment for persons with disabilities.

Building on the success of the "Hire the Handicapped" movement that provided some financial independence, persons with disabilities began to demand other rights.

Chapter 8 summarizes the story of the disability rights movement. As with many other civil rights stories, a few brave people had grown tired of the way they were treated, including being dependent on charity. In Toledo, the Toledo Society for Crippled Children became the Toledo Society for the Handicapped in 1974, and then the Ability Center of Greater Toledo, a center for independent living. Today, the Ability Center celebrates its ninetieth birthday not as an organization seeking charity for its clients, but instead as a strong advocate pushing the community to support the right of disabled people to live independently.

The last chapter examines what the term "disabled" means today when medical science can make some disabilities invisible. Yet those same medical miracles that "cure" disability also allow the able-bodied to live longer, leaving most of us to face almost certain infirmity at some time in our lives. These changes in whom we define as disabled and how we define disability will undoubtedly impact our future understanding of the history of disability.

A word on terminology used to describe various disabilities throughout the book—because this is an historical examination of disability, it includes words that are seen today as demeaning, such as "imbecile," "retarded," "crippled," "feebleminded," and "handicapped." These words are used only as they fit the historical context of the time, and certainly no insults are intended. This terminology reveals much about how society viewed the disabled throughout our history. A terminology timeline appendix is included.

The preface is written by Dr. Jim Ferris, the Ability Center of Greater Toledo Endowed Chair in Disability Studies. The Ward M. Canaday Center for Special Collections looks forward to continuing our relationship with the Disability Studies Program and building collections that will expand the knowledge of disability history. By educating future generations of students in Disability Studies, Dr. Ferris will help to ensure that the history of disability in our community will not be forgotten.

Chapter 1

ATTICS, ALMSHOUSES, AND ASYLUMS
Care for People with Mental Illness

By Kimberly Brownlee

We have endeavored to put forth every effort for the cure of disease and use every means at our command for diverting patients from their morbid fancies and directing their thoughts into natural and healthy channels, believing that in this line lies the most important factors for restoring diseased brains to their normal functions.

Dr. H.A. Tobey, superintendent of the
Toledo State Hospital, 1895

In colonial America, mental illness was believed to be caused by demonic possession, witchcraft, or sinful behavior, and was therefore considered something to be punished. Often the mentally ill were chained in basements or attics of almshouses and jails, or even in their own homes. Others roamed the streets of their communities and survived as best they could. The responsibility for the care of the mentally ill fell primarily upon families, churches, and communities. Living conditions in almshouses were often appalling; medical care was practically non-existent. Treatment, if given at all, most commonly involved blood-letting, the administration of opiates, the use of physical restraints, or dosing with purgatives.

This changed at the beginning of the nineteenth century when the concept of the "moral treatment" of the mentally ill became accepted. Moral treatment was based on the belief that insanity was the result of damage caused by a person's environment. By removing the person from that environment, he or she might have a chance to recover. Moral treatment advocated treating mentally ill persons with sympathy and kindness, in a place away from family, stress, and the overstimulation of modern society. Medical treatment and a clean, healthy atmosphere, with good food, fresh air, productive work, exercise, and education were the key elements of rehabilitation.

Yet despite these advances, this time was not without its own untoward practices for treating mentally ill people. Whirling and rotating devices were sometimes used to calm patients' nerves. Patients were sometimes branded with hot irons or submerged in cold water to bring them to their senses. Early in the 1840s, Dorothea Dix, a Massachusetts Sunday School teacher who had taught female inmates in the East Cambridge jail, undertook a survey of places in her state where the mentally ill were housed. Eventually, she expanded her investigation to include states from New Hampshire to Louisiana. She found conditions deplorable and abuse commonplace.

In her testimony to Massachusetts state legislators about care provided to the mentally ill, Dix stated, "I proceed, gentlemen, briefly to call your attention to the *present* state of insane persons confined within this Commonwealth, in *cages, closets, cellars, stalls, pens! Chained, naked, beaten with rods*, and *lashed* into obedience."[1] Dix began advocating for more humane treatment of the mentally ill. She pushed for the construction and expansion of psychiatric hospitals so that more patients could be taken out of poorhouses and jails and placed where they could receive proper treatment. As a result of her work, many new hospitals were built and the living conditions of thousands improved.

While progress was made, many people with mental illness were still being kept in jails and other less-than-desirable situations. Dix reported, "Feeble minds, too infirm of purpose to keep in the straight path, too incapable of reasoning out their truest good and best interests, and many, of constitutionally depraved propensities, these, chiefly, fill the cells of our Penitentiaries."[2] During the period following the Civil War, social reformers began to pressure states to take responsibility for the care of their mentally ill citizens and advocated for the building of asylums. The states responded and often built hospitals in rural areas with farmland. Patients helped work the farms and provided much of the asylums' food supplies.

The moral treatment approach continued to be used, with some success, into the early twentieth century. This period also saw great increases in immigration and urbanization. People began moving from the country into the cities and were no longer able to care for their sick or aged relatives who were left at state mental hospitals. Hospitals soon became overcrowded, often caring for people with disabilities other than mental illness. While originally intended to provide a pastoral atmosphere where patients could recover in a healthy, clean, stress-free environment, the hospitals became a source of stress themselves. Conditions deteriorated, and the practice of using physical restraints to subdue patients returned as a way to deal with overcrowding.[3]

Toledo's Early Care for the Mentally Ill

In Toledo, early care of persons with mental illness fell to the Lucas County Poor Farm, later renamed the County Infirmary. The poor farm was an idea dating back to the state's 1803 founding, when township trustees were authorized to appoint an "overseer of the poor" to provide "outdoor relief" to the needy. This often came in the form of money, food, medical care, fuel, or clothing. By the time Lucas County was founded in 1835, responsibility for caring for the needy had shifted to the counties, and the state authorized county commissioners to build poor houses. In January 1838, the Lucas County commissioners appointed a committee to locate and acquire a site for a county poor farm, and by April they had purchased the north half of Section 16, Township No. 3, located at the southeast corner of Detroit and Arlington. The commissioners appropriated $1,000 to develop it into a poor farm.[4]

The Lucas County Poor Farm sustained many of society's outcasts, including those with mental illness, the infirm, persons with disabilities, "friendless" elderly, epileptics, paupers, alcoholics, and others who could not support themselves. In exchange, those receiving support who were physically and/or mentally able were required to work on the farm, maintaining the grounds, growing crops, caring for livestock, and performing other needed tasks.

Even after Lucas County opened its poor farm, many of the county's residents with mental illness were still being kept in local jails. As late as 1854, the county commissioners appointed an individual to "take charge of the Jail at Maumee City, for the purpose of receiving . . . insane persons, and perhaps some County paupers."[5] In 1861, the commissioners voted to build an asylum on the grounds of the County Infirmary (as the Poor Farm was then called), saying that they considered it "inhuman and brutal" to continue to keep those with mental illness in jails.[6] The small, one-story asylum building was occupied by the fall of that year. At that time, the infirmary consisted of 115 acres, 83 of which were cultivated, and the patients were raising hay, oats, produce, and pork, as well as other livestock.

In 1867, the state legislature created the Ohio Board of State Charities, whose mission was to "investigate the whole system of the public charitable and correctional institutions of the state" and to "recommend such changes and additional provisions as they may deem necessary."[7] Upon investigating the Lucas County Infirmary in 1868, the board found conditions to be inadequate. Its 1868 report noted: "Visited Lucas County Infirmary . . . and shared, no doubt, fully in the mortification experienced at the general condition of the premises and the inmates. The buildings are more at fault than the management, yet the latter could be greatly improved. Ten small rooms, illy ventilated and wholly comfortless in appearance, constitute the full capacity of the Infirmary buildings proper. . . . The insane building is of brick, small, and without the least adaptation to its use. In it, the insane, epileptic and idiotic are kept indiscriminately as to age, sex or condition."[8]

Apparently the county took the board's comments to heart. After its subsequent inspection in 1871, the board reported that the infirmary had "undergone very marked improvement in its buildings and management. The repulsive features of the place, reported on a former occasion, have disappeared altogether. That further improvement ought to be made, and some additional care given that would still further improve the household is still quite apparent, but that these will come in due time, no one who judges from the past can doubt."[9]

Despite efforts to improve care for mentally ill persons, the Board of State Charities reported in 1870 that there were still almost 1,200 in the state's infirmaries and jails. The new asylum on the Lucas County Infirmary grounds, however, was not yet finished. This new asylum, named the Northwestern Hospital for the Insane, was completed in 1871. The new building was intended to "succeed the Lucas County Asylum," the small building constructed a decade earlier.[10] It was described as "an elegant and quite commodious brick structure, three stories high, and capable of accomdating [sic] from 75 to 100 patients."[11] Although it was a county institution, it was heavily funded by the state in exchange for accepting overflow patients from other state hospitals. The facility continued operating through the late 1880s, but ceased to exist sometime between 1887 and 1890, probably due to the opening of the Toledo Asylum for the Insane (Toledo State Hospital) in 1888. In its 1887 annual report, the board stated, "The completion of the State Asylum at Toledo, will possibly obviate the further employment of the care hitherto provided in this asylum. That its accommodations may still be required, is, however, probable."[12]

In 1878, the Board of State Charities reported that the Lucas County Infirmary's "buildings are . . . ill-suited to their use, but, at present, in good hands, and under careful management." It also reported that the Northwestern Hospital for the Insane was being "wisely and kindly managed."[13] In 1886, the board stated that the infirmary had 240 acres, and that "a kind care [was being] exercised by the immediate management."[14] The following year, the board reported that the hospital's superintendent, Dr. A.B. Wright, "has been faithful to his trust, as his house and household would attest to the most casual visitor,"[15] and the year after that, mentioned that a fire had originated in the laundry facility and had threatened the main building, but "by prompt and well directed efforts of the superintendent and employes [sic]," had been extinguished before causing what could have been a tragedy. The report added, "Great praise is due Dr. Wright and his assistants for their heroic fight with the flames."[16]

In 1898, the Lucas County General Hospital was built on the infirmary's grounds and in 1911, a tuberculosis hospital was added. The infirmary's facilities eventually included five buildings—the County Home, the general and tuberculosis hospitals, and two men's buildings. One author wrote that "it constantly cares for some 300 sick, infirm, insane, epileptic and idiotic people."[17] In 1931, a new building, the Lucas County Hospital, replaced the General Hospital and in 1937, the William Roche Tuberculosis Sanatorium replaced the old Tuberculosis Hospital.

In 1944, the Lucas County Hospital, previously overseen by the county commissioners, was put under the management of a board of trustees and thus cut its connection to the county. Its name was changed to Maumee Valley Hospital. In 1950, a new home was opened at the infirmary called the Lucas County Home for the Aged; in 1969, this home merged with Maumee Valley Hospital and became the Maumee Valley Hospital Long-Term Care Unit. It provided extended care services to the hospital's patients. By 1970, the hospital was experiencing debilitating financial problems and was sold to the Medical College of Ohio. MCO took over management of the hospital, operating it until 1980, when it vacated the building and moved to its new facility on Arlington Avenue. The structure that was the County Hospital still stands, and it was in this building that MCO's physician-training program began. By 2000, Lucas County commissioners again had control of the structure and converted it to apartments for low-income senior citizens.[18]

The Toledo State Hospital

By 1883, severe overcrowding in Ohio's existing psychiatric hospitals and the fact that over 1,000 of the state's citizens with mental illness continued to be housed in jails necessitated building an additional asylum. On April 18, the Ohio General Assembly formed a commission to locate a suitable site for a new asylum remote from its existing facilities for the insane.[19] The commission consisted of the governor, attorney general, secretary of state, auditor, and General Roehliff Brinkerhoff, a member of the Board of State Charities.

After much research and study, the commission selected a site at the southwest corner of Arlington and Detroit avenues, across the street from the Lucas County Infirmary. The county offered to donate 150 acres for the project; the city of Toledo agreed to supply water at the cost of pumping, and the local gas company offered to provide natural gas at a greatly reduced rate. The land was well-suited for such a project—it was bordered by Swan Creek, well-drained, and had fertile soil suitable for farming.

The state made it clear that it could only appropriate $500,000 for the project and it required that the finished facility be able to accommodate at least 650 patients. General Brinkerhoff was a strong advocate of the "detached ward system," also known as the "cottage system." He was convinced they could build such a facility at a much lower price than one based on the previously popular and traditional Kirkbride design, where patients were housed in attached pavilions. The commission members studied the options and visited three other states where the detached ward system was used. In the end, they voted to adopt the newer, revolutionary system for the Toledo facility.

The hospital's buildings were designed by prominent Toledo architect Edward O. Fallis, who designed other important Toledo buildings, including the Valentine Theater. The original plans called for thirty-four structures including twenty cottages, two strong wards, two infirm wards, two hospitals, an administration building, a chapel, a kitchen and bakery, a laundry, a storehouse, a boiler house, and two dining halls. Each cottage had a different architectural design in order to create a domestic setting. Deliberate effort was made to eliminate any prison-like appearance, common in older designs. In fact, the buildings and park-like grounds of the Toledo State Hospital were so beautiful that they were frequently pictured on postcards and were often the setting of family picnics and other outings.

The original estimated cost was $564,000, but during the construction process some changes to the original plans were necessary; some structures were damaged by a tornado. The commission asked for an additional $292,000 for the changes and repairs. In the end, construction of the facility cost $750,000. Thanks to the commissioners' innovative ideas, however, the finished facility was able to accommodate over 1,000 patients and 200 employees. Construction and furnishing of the new asylum cost around $700 per capita, compared to an average of around $1,100 per capita for construction of traditional asylums.

The asylum opened in January 1888, with Dr. Henry A. Tobey serving as superintendent. The first patients were mostly transfers from other facilities in the state. The methods used for treating persons with mental illnesses were changing, and the cottage model fit well into the new approach because of its home-like atmosphere and freedom, thought to produce a sense of self-worth and independence. Tobey believed that meaningful employment, diversion, recreation, regimentation, freedom, and privileges were the best methods for restoring the "mentally disturbed." Physical restraints were rarely used.

The admitted individuals suffered from a wide variety of mental and physical illnesses and behavioral changes. Among the causes of insanity noted in patient records were syphilis, dementia, epilepsy, alcoholism, old age, psychosis with mental deficiency, and head injury. Other causes noted were more unusual: "religious excitement," "marriage," "jealousy," "sexual self abuse," "political excitement," "prostitution," "lactation," "seduction," "financial trouble," and "loss of pension."[20]

Patients were initially admitted to one of the hospital buildings, but as their conditions improved, they were transferred to the cottages. As at the county infirmary, asylum patients who could work did so. Male patients did much of the work on the new grounds—planting trees and flowers, sowing grass, building driveways, and excavating the six lagoons that were eventually part of the landscape. The female patients worked at crafts such as weaving and rug-making. Dr. Tobey wrote, "It has been our aim to give every patient as far as possible some healthful employment, believing that there is nothing more prejudicial to a person's well-being, sane or insane, than enforced idleness."[21]

Within the first ten years, the asylum's facilities increased to include a greenhouse, two hospital buildings, an auditorium, an animal slaughterhouse, an additional boiler house, and a two-acre lake. The lake added beauty to the grounds and also served as a source of ice and extra water. In addition, some of the patients took it upon themselves to stock it with fish. The hospital also formed a cornet band during this time. A medical library was added in the administration building; a water tower was built; and additions were made to the men's hospital, the greenhouse, and several cottages. A new men's hospital was also built, which increased the capacity of the institution to 1,500. In 1894, the Toledo Asylum for the Insane officially changed its name to the Toledo State Hospital.

By 1905, the hospital formed what was called "the best baseball team in Northwestern Ohio," made up of both patients and employees.[22] That year, the team lost only five out of thirty-six games played on the grounds. Patients continued to raise their own vegetables and fruits on 240 acres of land, and with the addition of hog pens and fences, they were also able to raise their own pork. In 1906, Dr. Tobey retired, and members of the Board of Superintendents passed a resolution expressing their sadness at his departure after so many years of service.

The minutes from March 16 read: "Resolved, that in the opinion of the members of this Board, the beneficent influence of the faithful, competent and persistent endeavor of this eminent scholar and gentleman, in developing and promoting a high standard of proficiency, what is known as the Cottage System, will be felt as a blessing to mankind, and will prove a monument to the philanthropy and capability of this kind hearted friend of his race whom the world owes a debt of gratitude and affection."[23] Dr. George R. Love replaced Tobey as superintendent.

Following World War I, an increase in the awareness of mental illness and improvements in its treatment resulted in overcrowding at the hospital. At the same time, the hospital changed its admission policy to allow individuals who sought treatment to commit themselves and circumvent the former, required court process. Previously, individuals who wanted help but did not wish to go through the courts did not receive treatment. To cope with the overcrowding problem, neurosyphilis and mental hygiene clinics were started and a women's hospital was built, increasing the institution's capacity to 1,600. The hospital also began providing outpatient services to individuals from the community and former patients. During this time, a beauty shop and a retail outlet for patients' crafts were added.

In 1919, Love was succeeded by Dr. O.O. Fordyce as superintendent. Treatment methods were also changing and included hydro, occupational, and psychological therapy. A school of nursing, operated in conjunction with the Lucas County Hospital, became fully accredited before closing during World War II because of personnel shortages.

In the 1930s, the hospital added a new employee cafeteria and a variety of clinics that were supervised by consulting physicians. Publication of a hospital newspaper called "To-Sta-Ho" began and a patient library was established. Also during this decade, a nine-hole golf course was added and maintained by the patients; many tournaments between patients and employees were held. In 1939, the average daily patient population was over 2,700.

In the early 1940s, the hospital conducted a study and determined that its optimum capacity was 2,054, making it mandatory to restrict admissions. But patient admissions again increased, due to World War II-related stress, while the number of nurses decreased as many left to serve in the military. During this period, the hospital tried to grow as much food as possible to aid in the war effort. It cultivated over 1,000 acres, acquired a dairy herd, and increased its production of poultry and pork.

After the war, admissions again increased because of an influx of aged persons. The hospital began using electric shock therapy, claiming a sixty-one percent success rate for improvement. New drug treatments were also used for various forms of psychosis, particularly insulin and Metrazol. In 1946, Dr. J.E. Duty succeeded Fordyce as superintendent, and in 1948, construction began on a new receiving hospital.

During the 1950s, the patient population peaked at over 3,000. Fortunately, the new receiving hospital could hold 220 patients; an additional wing was built two years later, adding eighty-four beds. A co-ed cottage for geriatric patients opened, and the old water tower was converted into the hospital's post office. Treatment options increased with the development of new drugs that improved patients' conditions. There was still a shortage of doctors and nurses, but the hospital began to give support personnel more extensive training and responsibilities, previously handled only by nurses.

By the 1960s, patient treatment mainly consisted of tranquilizers and individual or group therapy. Electric shock therapy was still used occasionally. Some of the hospital's buildings had become unsafe for occupancy and were demolished. A new kitchen, bakery, and employee cafeteria replaced the original; the dairy operation was eliminated when the herd was transferred to another state institution. The hospital operated several outpatient clinics to help patients ease back into life in their respective communities after leaving the hospital. These clinics were held each month at Lima, Defiance, Sandusky, and Toledo. There was also an "after-care clinic" located in the receiving hospital on the grounds.

In 1971, the hospital's name was changed to the Toledo Mental Health Center, and during the next twenty years, the number of patients it treated dropped from over 3,000 to around 300. Advancements in psychotropic medications, an increase in outpatient services, and the availability of individual and group therapy at other hospitals and in the community made the decrease possible. As the number of patients declined and structures emptied, they were razed.[24] A new state-supported facility, Northwest Ohio Psychiatric Hospital, formerly the Toledo Mental Health Center, now operates on the site, providing adult psychiatric care. Today, all of the original buildings of the old state hospital are gone. All that is visible of the once bucolic grounds and grand facility that served so many people in the midst of their personal sufferings are a few of the original lagoons.

The people who came to the Toledo State Hospital for help suffered during a time when treatment of mental illness was still much of a mystery. Some recovered and were able to return to society. Others came and went several times. Still others were admitted and never left. Many who died at the hospital were claimed by family or friends and buried privately. But almost 2,000 who died at the hospital were buried in two cemeteries on the hospital grounds. Their graves are visible only as rows of depressions in the ground. They are marked by stones smaller than the size of bricks and display only patient numbers. Many of these have sunk into the ground. The cemeteries themselves are now noted with official state historical markers. While it is fitting that these individuals remain at rest on the former hospital grounds, the fact that their individual graves are not marked with their names and their burial places little noted is also a commentary on their lives—lives that society forgot.

A cemetery reclamation committee now works to locate each of the graves and raise the sunken stones to make them visible again. By doing so, the committee hopes to return, or perhaps for the first time, bring dignity, honor, and respect to those who are buried there.

Endnotes

1. Dorothea L. Dix, "Memorial to the Legislature of Massachusetts, 1843," reproduced in Marvin Rosen, Gerald R. Clark, and Marvin S. Kivitz, *The History of Mental Retardation: Collected Papers* (Baltimore, University Park Press, 1976), vol. 1, 6.
2. D. L. Dix, *Remarks on Prisons and Prison Discipline in the United States*, University Park Press (Boston, Munroe & Francis, 1845), 61.
3. For more information on early treatment of the mentally ill, see: Walter Bromberg, *From Shaman to Psychotherapist: A History of the Treatment of Mental Illness* (Chicago, H. Regney, 1975); and Donna R. Kemp, *Mental Health in America: A Reference Handbook* (Santa Barbara, California, ABC-CLIO, 2007).
4. Clark Waggoner, ed., *History of the City of Toledo and Lucas County, Ohio* (New York, Munsell & Company 1888), part 1, 314.
5. Waggoner, part 1, 316.
6. Waggoner, part 1, 317.
7. Ohio Legislature, "An Act in Relation to State Charitable and Correctional Institutions," reproduced in Ohio Board of State Charities, *Third Annual Report to the Governor of the State of Ohio for the Year 1869* (Columbus, Ohio, L.D. Myers & Bros., State Printers, 1870).
8. Ohio Board of State Charities, *Second Annual Report to the Governor of the State of Ohio for the Year 1868* (Columbus, Ohio, L.D. Myers & Bros., State Printers, 1869), 51-52.
9. Ohio Board of State Charities, *Fifth Annual Report to the Governor of the State of Ohio for the Year 1871* (Columbus, Ohio, L.D. Myers & Bros., State Printers, 1872), 48.
10. Waggoner, part 1, 11.
11. Ohio Board of State Charities, *Fifth Annual Report*, 48.
12. Ohio Board of State Charities, *Twelfth Annual Report to the 68th General Assembly of the State of Ohio for the Fiscal Year Ending November 15, 1887* (Columbus, Ohio, L.D. Myers & Bros., State Printers, 1888), 33.
13. Ohio Board of State Charities, *Second Annual Report to the General Assembly of Ohio for the Year 1877* (Columbus, Ohio, L.D. Myers & Bros., State Printers, 1878), 38.
14. Ohio Board of State Charities, *Tenth Annual Report to the Sixty-Seventh General Assembly for the Fiscal Year Ending November 15, 1885* (Columbus, Ohio, L.D. Myers & Bros., State Printers, 1886), 68.
15. Ohio Board of State Charities, *Eleventh Annual Report to the Sixty-Seventh General Assembly for the Fiscal Year Ending November 15, 1886* (Columbus, Ohio, L.D. Myers & Bros., State Printers, 1887), 35.
16. Ohio Board of State Charities, *Twelfth Annual Report*, 33.
17. Harvey Scribner, ed., *Memoirs of Lucas County and the City of Toledo* (Madison, Wisconsin, Western Historical Association, 1910), 109.

18. For more information on the history of the Lucas County Infirmary, Northwestern Hospital for the Insane, and Maumee Valley Hospital, see: Walter Hartung, *History of Medical Practice in Toledo and the Maumee Valley Area 1600-1990* (Toledo, privately printed, 1992), 121-123; John M. Killets, ed., *Toledo and Lucas County, Ohio 1623-1923* (Chicago—The S.J. Clarke Publishing Company, 1923) vol. 1, 605-606; Harvey Scribner, ed., *Memoirs of Lucas County and the City of Toledo* (Madison, Wisconsin, Western Historical Association, 1910) vol. 1, 109, 257; and Clark Waggoner, *History of the City of Toledo and Lucas County, Ohio* (New York Munsell & Company, 1888) pt. 1, 11, 314, 316-317, 325.
19. Ohio Legislature, "An Act to provide for additional accommodations for the Insane of the State," reproduced in Board of Trustees and Officers of the Toledo Asylum for the Insane, *First Annual Report of the Board of Trustees and Officers of the Toledo Asylum for the Insane to the Governor of the State of Ohio for the Year 1884* (Columbus, Ohio, Westbote Co., State Printers, 1885), 5-6.
20. Board of Trustees and Officers of the Toledo Asylum for the Insane, *Annual Report[s] of the Board of Trustees and Officers of the Toledo Asylum for the Insane to the Governor of the State of Ohio* (Columbus, Ohio, Westbote Co., State Printers, various dates).
21. Board of Trustees and Officers of the Toledo Asylum for the Insane, *Sixth Annual Report of the Board of Trustees and Officers of the Toledo Asylum for the Insane to the Governor of the State of Ohio for the Fiscal Year Ending November 15, 1889* (Columbus, Ohio, 1890), 14.
22. Hartung, 114.
23. Toledo State Hospital, Board of Trustees Minutes, March 16, 1906. The Ohio State Archives, Series 968, Ohio Historical Society.
24. For more information on the history of the Toledo State Hospital, see: Roeliff Brinkerhoff, *Recollections of a Lifetime* (Cincinnati, Ohio, The Robert Clarke Company, 1900) 242-254; and Clyde Cox, *History of Toledo State Hospital 1888-1964* (typescript, Toledo-Lucas County Public Library, 1964); Hartung, 111-119; Killets, vol. 1, 608-609; Scribner, vol. 1, 257-259; and Waggoner, part 1, 562.

Patients on the front porch of one of the cottages, Toledo State Hospital, 1890

Dr. Henry A. Tobey,
first superintendent of the Toledo State Hospital
(From Sharon Yaros)

Hon. Board of Trustees of
The Toledo Asylum for the Insane
  Gentlemen:
    I am in receipt of a communication from your Secretary, Mr Walter Pickens, notifying me of your action of the 17th inst., electing me to the honorable position of Superintendent of the Asylum under your control.
    I accept the position with many thanks to you, Gentlemen, for the confidence you have reposed in me, and do so, I trust, fully realizing the great responsibilities imposed upon me, and my obligations to you, to the public, and to the unfortunates that will be committed to our care.
    With great respect I am
      Very truly Yours
        H. A. Tobey

Lima Ohio
  Nov. 25th 1886

Dr. H. A. Tobey's letter of acceptance for the position of superintendent of the Toledo Asylum for the Insane, 1886

Women's Hospital, the Toledo State Hospital
(From the Toledo-Lucas County Public Library)

Dorothea Dix

General Roehliff Brinkerhoff, proponent of the "cottage system" for the Toledo State Hospital

The first annual report, which predates the construction of the hospital

The Northwestern Hospital for the Insane (From the Toledo-Lucas County Public Library)

LIST OF BILLS OF FARE

FOR THE

ASSOCIATE DINING ROOMS

OF THE

TOLEDO STATE HOSPITAL

For one week of each month during the Fiscal Year ending November 15th, 1894.

AND ALSO A LIST OF THE

AMUSEMENTS AND ENTERTAINMENTS

GIVEN DURING THE SAME PERIOD.

The menu and activities scheduled at the hospital in November 1894

The 1905 baseball team of the Toledo State Hospital (From the Toledo-Lucas County Public Library)

Postcard of the Chapel and Administration Building of the Toledo State Hospital (From Sharon Yaros)

A marker on a grave at one of the state hospital cemeteries (From Sharon Yaros)

Aerial view of the Toledo State Hospital grounds, ca. 1950s.

The Lucas County Infirmary and Hospital (From Sharon Yaros)

Chapter 2

SHELTERED WORKSHOPS AND SOCIAL CLUBS
Services for Vision and Hearing Impaired Persons

By Jennifer Free

That evening there was a large meeting, including Rotarians and Feilbach teachers, where Miss Keller, blind and deaf, asked for funds to continue work for the blind. Miss Anne Sullivan, her wonderful teacher who taught Miss Keller to speak, showed how Miss Keller could understand what people said although she was deaf. She put fingers on both sides of the person's nose, on their lips, and on the throat to get the vibrations of the speaker's voice. Rev. Allen Stockdale was told to say something to demonstrate that she did understand him. She put her fingers at the sides of his nose, on his lips and throat. Then he said, "Every man in the audience is jealous of me."

Recollection of Helen Keller's visit to Toledo, 1925.

Blind persons have often suffered greater stigmatization than others with disabilities because they were unwelcome reminders of the fragility of eyesight. Three strands of stigmatization about blindness run through history: blindness as a social liability, blindness as punishment for sin, and blindness as uselessness to self and others.[1] Because of society's perceptions of those who were blind, they were often cloistered at home because they reflected badly on their families.

Deaf persons, too, suffered discrimination, especially those who were born deaf. Their lack of speech led many to believe they were developmentally disabled, and the congenitally deaf were referred to as "deaf and dumb." Deaf persons living in urban areas formed close-knit communities, usually centered around social clubs. Society tried to assimilate them into the hearing world by stressing oralism (teaching the deaf to communicate primarily or exclusively through lip-reading and speaking rather than signing) over sign language, but many resisted because they felt it meant giving up their cultural identity and community.

The image of blind and deaf persons changed at the turn of the twentieth century when the story of Helen Keller, who lost her vision and hearing in infancy, became widely known with the 1903 publication of her autobiography, *The Story of My Life*.[2] Keller's dramatic story began in 1887 when Anne Sullivan was hired by the Keller family of Alabama to educate their six-year-old child. Sullivan, herself vision impaired, taught Keller to read and write Braille, use a typewriter, and speak. Keller went on to earn a college degree from Radcliffe College, the first blind and deaf person in the country to do so. She became a nationally-known celebrity and was friends with many famous people, including Alexander Graham Bell, Charlie Chaplin, and Mark Twain. Mark Twain was quoted as saying, "the two most interesting characters of the nineteenth century are Napoleon and Helen Keller."[3]

Keller became the torchbearer for causes supporting blind persons. If Helen Keller could succeed, others with vision and hearing impairments could, too. The American Foundation for the Blind, founded in 1921 to "work for the blind, partially blind, and to do such things as are not, or cannot be done, by existing agencies," had achieved some success in gaining services for persons with vision impairment, including a federal subsidy for the American Printing House for the Blind. Capitalizing on Keller's and Sullivan's popularity, the organization hired the two women to raise funds. In 1924 and 1925, they visited fifty-three cities and gave 139 speeches, including one at the Feilbach School for Crippled Children in Toledo.[4] While the tour fell short of the foundation's fundraising goals, Keller became a star, and her promotion of blind and deaf issues raised public consciousness.

Ohio's Efforts to Assist Blind Persons

Education for blind children was an early concern of American society, and many residential schools were established in the first half of the nineteenth century. Between 1832 and 1833, schools for blind children opened in New York, Boston, and Philadelphia, funded by philanthropists and operated as charitable organizations. By the time of the American Civil War, eighteen additional residential schools opened.

Ohio was one of the first states to recognize that education for blind citizens was a public responsibility. At a convention of medical experts in Columbus in 1835, attendees advocated for a public asylum for the instruction of the blind. At that time, the total number of visually impaired Ohioans was estimated at approximately 250.

In 1836, Dr. William Awl, who had attended the Columbus convention, traveled to New York to view an exhibit coordinated by officials and students of the Institution for the Blind of New York. After watching the presentation, Awl decided Ohio, too, should have such an institution. Back in Columbus, he drafted a resolution for the Ohio General Assembly calling for the collection of data necessary to justify the creation of a school for blind persons.

In addition to the resolution, Awl and his associates distributed approximately 2,000 pamphlets to justices of the peace in every township in the state, requesting statistics on the number of blind people in their townships. In 1836, the Ohio legislature appointed a board of trustees—which included Awl and Noah Swayne, a Toledo lawyer—to study how best to educate blind people in the state. As a result of the board's efforts, on April 3, 1837, the assembly authorized the appropriation of funds to establish the Ohio Institution for the Education of the Blind. It was to be a residential school open to any visually impaired or blind child between the ages of three and twenty-one who was a permanent resident of Ohio. The Ohio institution was the first state-supported school of its kind in the United States.

On July 4, 1837, the Institution opened its doors in a rented facility with a prayer service attended by over 900 people in downtown Columbus. The number of students enrolled was small, just eleven. Ten years later, the total number of students accepted had climbed to 150, with fifty-five students graduating during the decade. Female students were taught domestic skills; male students received vocational training that allowed them to find gainful employment after graduation. Many graduates pursued careers assisting other blind persons. Samuel Bacon, an 1846 graduate, opened the Illinois Institution for the Blind and went on to become its superintendent for eight years.

As ideas about the appropriate education for students evolved, the school's curriculum changed accordingly. In 1897, a typewriting course was offered for the first time, opening up new vocational options for the students. In 1903, the trustees appropriated $10,000 for the construction of two gymnasiums, as the curriculum moved toward a more holistic view of education. Instructors sought to narrow the divide between education offered to sighted students and that offered to visually impaired and blind students.

In the early 1900s, the institution was renamed the Ohio State School for the Blind. Control was transferred from the Ohio Department of Public Welfare to the Ohio Department of Education, showing the clear intent of the administrators to coordinate the education of the blind with that of fully sighted students. The school physically moved in 1953 to another site in Columbus in order to expand its offerings and to serve more students.

Services for Blind Persons in Northwest Ohio

While the state of Ohio founded its school in the early nineteenth century, services for the vision impaired in Toledo did not begin until 1923. In October of that year, members of the Toledo Lions Club approached the Community Chest, the local fundraising organization (and predecessor to the United Way), requesting services to help Toledo's blind citizens. The Toledo club was part of the Lions Clubs International, a philanthropic organization founded in 1917 to promote civic welfare. The Toledo club was ahead of the international organization in advocating for assistance to visually impaired persons. The Lions Clubs International did not adopt blindness as its philanthropic focus until 1925, after Helen Keller addressed the international convention at Cedar Point in Sandusky, and challenged the group to become "knights of the blind in the crusade against darkness."[5]

The Toledo Community Chest employed Dr. Harry Wills, former professor of sociology at the University of Toledo, to conduct a survey of blind persons residing in the Toledo area to determine if there was an identifiable need for a city organization to provide services for the vision impaired. The survey results indicated that such a group was both necessary and desirable. Edward Evans and Frank Saxton, members of the local Chamber of Commerce, pledged their support, and along with several prominent Toledoans, they appeared before the Community Chest's board of directors to request funds to organize a society for blind persons. After several meetings, the Community Chest agreed to fund the organization. The group was originally named the Toledo Committee of the American Federation for the Blind, with Harry Wills as its first executive secretary.

In January 1924, the Toledo Committee of the American Federation for the Blind was reorganized as the Toledo Society for the Blind, and Edward E. Evans was chosen as its first president. The group's articles of incorporation stated its purpose was "to care for and assist the blind and to further the interests of the blind and to open all possible avenues to independence and self support, through investigation, education, and recreation."[6] The Community Chest allocated $1,500; the Social Services Foundation donated office space in their downtown building. It soon became apparent that the Society needed a larger space if it wanted to promote and organize social clubs and other group functions. Five months later, the Society moved its office to Huron Street where it rented two rooms in another office building. The Happy Times Club (for women) and the Progressive Club (for men and women) were formed at this time. The organization also offered free classes in basket-weaving and chair-caning for members. For many participants, these vocational skills became their first source of income. The products produced by members sold quickly.

The organization outgrew its offices again, and in 1925, relocated to a large hall in the Valentine Building to facilitate social and recreational activities. Popular dance classes for all ages were offered. The Society held its first annual picnic and Christmas party, traditions that continued for many years. The number of blind residents in Toledo was estimated at about 300, but this number was likely low because some parents objected to their children being called blind if they had any vision, even limited.

In 1927, the Toledo Society for the Blind incorporated as a nonprofit corporation with the stated purpose "to further the interests of the blind and open to them all avenues to independence and self-support, through investigation, education, and recreation."[7] A $10,000 bequest from the Edward D. Libbey estate in 1928 allowed the Society to purchase a ten-room office on Michigan Street as the agency's headquarters. The space required extensive renovations, and Lions Club members volunteered to complete the task.

An issue of concern to supporters and members of the club was creating additional opportunities for vocational education. To fill that need, the Society opened its first sheltered workshop where members did rug-weaving on a loom donated by the Business and Professional Women's Club. John Richey, a blind weaver, taught clients and filled weaving orders. Other early workshop activities included making rubber mats, stringing tags, and making hospital sponges. In 1928, a donation from the estate of Toledoan Noah Swayne (one of the original trustees of the Ohio State Institution for the Blind) funded a workshop building. As a result of the Swayne bequest, all debt on the Society's property was paid and a trust fund was established.

Financial stability did not last long, however, as during the Depression, the Society's finances were severely strained. Its monthly check from the Community Chest was reduced to $150 from $400. A. Estelle Parsons, the Society's executive secretary, voluntarily agreed to a reduction in pay. Because workshop wages were inadequate for workers to support a family, the organization began providing a noon meal free of charge, and the Society frequently made loans—most of which were repaid in full once economic conditions improved. During this period, the Society supplied eyeglasses, paid part of its clients' hospital expenses when possible, and financed proper burials for many who had no savings or insurance. In addition, it collected and distributed surplus food and other basic necessities that the federal government donated. The Toledo chapter of the Red Cross provided vital aid to Society members during this time by supplying blankets and underwear.

Changes in federal law during the Depression permitted blind persons to become vendors in federal buildings. In 1936, the Toledo Society for the Blind placed Thomas Whitaker ("Blind Tom") in a newsstand in the Old Post Office Building; Blind Tom became well-known to downtown office workers. The next year, to deal with the difficulties disabled people experienced in finding employment, the Society began teaching independent living skills to make it easier for its clients to live in the sighted world. It purchased a house on Michigan Street where four to five blind individuals lived independently. The residents paid the rent, gas, and light bills, and the Society supplied furniture and fuel during the winter months. This independent living project continued until 1945 when the property was sold.

Not only did the Society endeavor to open employment opportunities, it also sought equal access to cultural opportunities. In April 1936, the Ohio Commission for the Blind designated the Society as the distributor of Talking Book machines in northwest Ohio, providing a new means of education and entertainment. Talking Book machines were produced as a work relief project of President Franklin Roosevelt's New Deal program.[8] During the program's first year, over 100 machines were lent locally; Toledo's program was among the first in the United States. The Society also continued to provide recreational opportunities for its clients, including swimming lessons and a one-week summer camp for blind youths on Catawba Island.

During World War II, the Toledo Society for the Blind again expanded its workshop program as part of the civilian war effort, enlarging its physical space and employing many more workers. It secured a contract with the Ohio and Michigan Paper Company, which in turn allowed twenty men and women to be placed on regular eight-hour work days for two and a half years, where they earned between $25 and $30 per week. Between 1942 and 1945, workshop participants produced thousands of waterproof liners designed to protect disassembled Jeeps for shipment overseas. After the war ended, however, the majority of blind factory workers were laid off. Nationally, federal contracts with sheltered workshops for the blind plummeted from $8 million during the war, to $600,000 after the war.[9] In response, the Society attempted several experimental vocational projects, including repotting plants and making flats for greenhouses. But the workers could not work fast enough to earn a reasonable salary, and the Society was forced to abandon this project. It returned to rug-weaving and chair-caning as its main workshop products.

Recognizing the importance of proper parenting in raising vision impaired children, the Society helped create the Parents of the Visually Handicapped in the 1950s. This group pushed for educational facilities for visually-impaired children in the city, part of a growing national trend away from state residential schools and toward educating blind children in the local public education system. In 1953, the Junior League staged a production depicting the life of an average, middle-class American family with a blind pre-schooler, thus helping increase the understanding of the need for a normal family life and appropriate educational opportunities for visually impaired children.

In October 1954, the Society purchased land and a vacant building on Canton Street downtown, along with a sizeable gift of property from a friend of the Society that allowed the construction of a new building. The sidewalks, parking lots, seeing-eye dog exercise yard, fencing, and interior equipment were all paid for by the Lions Clubs of Toledo, and the lounge was funded by the Zonta Club. The new building was dedicated as the Edward E. Evans Building on June 17, 1956, in honor of the Society's first president.

In the early 1960s, the Society began its community outreach services, including New Eyes for the Needy, where volunteers collected and repaired discarded eyeglasses, then distributed them. In 1965, it began its Operation Lazy Eye program to identify the common condition (amblyopia) that, if left untreated, could result in permanent impairment. By January 1966, approximately 1,200 children had been screened for the condition as a direct result of the program. The Society also began to provide direct rehabilitative services in the 1960s. Several staff members received intensive training in the areas of mobility and rehabilitation; the Society converted the basement of its main facility into a training room to teach orientation and mobility skills. A model apartment was used to teach the skills necessary to live independently. The rehabilitation program was funded by a grant from the Ohio Bureau of Services for the Blind. Rehabilitation efforts were extended to children in 1982, with a dollhouse used to teach independent living skills.

In 1976, the Society began a self-study and petitioned the National Accreditation Council for Agencies Serving the Blind and Visually Handicapped (NAC) for accreditation, but the NAC voted a one-year deferment prior to awarding the accreditation. Two years later, the Society embarked on an extensive renovation of the main building's administrative and direct services areas and updated and expanded its social work, rehabilitation instruction, mobility training, and prevention of blindness services. As a result, it received NAC accreditation in 1978.

In June 1979, as a reflection of its broader mission, the Toledo Society for the Blind became the Sight Center. The organization wanted to emphasize that its services were not restricted to Toledo and that most of its clients had some degree of vision. Also that year, the organization began a Telecasette program that allowed blind clients to call after hours and receive up-to-date news recorded on tape over the phone. Further audio services were offered, beginning in April 1982, with "The Sight Center on the Air," a weekly radio program broadcast from Scott High School. Seven years later, the Sight Center Audio Network (SCAN) was launched. Here clients could hear *The Blade* and the *Bowling Green Sentinel Tribune* read in their entirety on the air. SCAN became the largest radio reading service in Ohio as listeners eventually had a choice of seven daily newspapers from twenty-three counties served by the Center, along with a sizeable selection of national and local magazines.

In 2003, as a result of its increased client load that stretched its financial resources, the Center was forced to decrease its service area to sixteen northwest Ohio counties. To reflect its smaller geographic focus, its name became The Sight Center of Northwest Ohio. Despite fiscal challenges, the following year the Center launched its "Building a Vision for the Future" capital campaign directed at raising $1.65 million to purchase land and construct a new services building. That new building opened in 2007 on Garden Lake Parkway in south Toledo.

The Ohio State School for the Deaf

State-supported education of deaf children began even before the Ohio school for the blind was founded. The Reverend James Hoge had been inspired by a letter he read from a Pennsylvania deaf institution, inviting Ohio to send its deaf children there to receive an education. In 1823, he undertook a survey to determine the number of deaf Ohioans. As a result of that counting, and at Hoge's urging, the state established an Asylum for the Education of the Deaf and Dumb in 1826. The name of the school was changed to "institution" from "asylum" the following year and a board of trustees was named to oversee its formation.

In 1828, the legislature appointed the Reverend Horatio N. Hubbell as superintendent and teacher. They sent him to the American Asylum in Hartford, Connecticut, for eighteen months to receive advanced training in sign language and new instructional methods. A school site on East Town Street in Columbus was chosen, but because the legislature was spending most of its funds to build canals, it was unable to build the facility immediately. Instead, the state authorized the board of trustees to rent a small house in Columbus for the school. It became the fifth residential facility for deaf students in the country.

While the school charged $80 per year to attend, the Ohio assembly mandated that a free education to one needy student from each of the state's nine judicial districts be provided. In 1834, a new school opened on the East Town Street land that included a barn and several outbuildings. The facility was designed to accommodate between sixty and eighty students who lived at the school, with a matron entrusted to oversee their after-school care.

Whether to teach lip reading or sign language was an early issue at the school. Superintendent Hubbell's 1838 annual report emphasized the importance of deaf education and espoused a clear preference for teaching sign language over oral communication. In 1844, the oral-manual debate took up a sizeable portion of the superintendent's annual report. The controversy erupted nationally when American educator Horace Mann, after observing an oral class in Germany, argued for its exclusive use in the United States as well. Hubbell, however, warned against drawing sweeping conclusions about the oral skills and pointed to the demonstrable advantages of a visual-gestural language system. During this period, the Ohio institution trained a significant number of deaf educators who worked at similar residential facilities throughout the country.

In the latter half of the nineteenth century, the Institution continued to make facility and instructional changes. Its crumbling main building was replaced in 1868. Significant changes were also made in the curriculum. The school hired deaf tradesmen to provide vocational instruction because hearing instructors often lacked the appropriate communication skills. In 1866, the first female instructor was hired and a sewing department was added for women students. For the men, printing, book binding, and the publication of a daily newspaper, *The Ohio Chronicle*, were added to the curriculum.

In 1870, the facility began providing instruction in lip reading and articulation, coinciding with the Conference at Milan where advocates of the oral approach pressed strong arguments in favor of its adoption internationally. Oralism had many supporters, including some of the biggest names of the late nineteenth and early twentieth century—Alexander Graham Bell, Thomas Edison, and Andrew Carnegie.[10] Many deaf people objected to oralism. They felt sign language defined their culture, and they opposed the attempt to assimilate them into the hearing world.

The beginning of the twentieth century saw the school's highest enrollment, with over 500 students on its roster. To reflect its emphasis on education, the Institution officially changed its name to the Ohio State School for the Deaf and its operation was transferred from the Department of Welfare to the Ohio Department of Education. By 1944, as concerns over the safety of the building were increasing, the board purchased 200 acres of land on the north side of Columbus for a new facility, which opened in 1953.

As with many state-run institutions, the federal 1975 Education for All Handicapped Children Act, mandating a "free and appropriate public education in the least restrictive environment," led to major changes for the deaf school.[11]

Enrollment at the state school decreased substantially as students were placed in local public schools.

Services for Deaf Persons in Toledo

The first school for deaf children in Toledo was founded in 1911. When the Charles Feilbach School for Crippled Children opened downtown in 1918, the Toledo School for the Deaf and Hard of Hearing moved into the building. Little is known of the school, and while it appears to have been supported by the Rotary Club of Toledo in the same manner that the Feilbach School was, there is no documentation of its programs in Rotary records.

Other early programs for deaf Toledoans included the Deaf Club. In the late nineteenth and early twentieth centuries, deaf persons began to define themselves as a distinct linguistic and cultural group; deaf clubs were popular as places to create a sense of community. The Toledo Deaf Club dates back to the 1930s and was originally called the Silent Club. In his book *Deaf Hearing Boy: A Memoir*, R.H. Miller described how his parents, both of whom were deaf, visited the club often to socialize. "My parents' social life revolved around a locale on Adams Street (now demolished) called the Toledo Silent Club, which provided a place where you have a drink or beer and hang out. Because it depended on a membership who had very little financial resources, it was a seedy, rundown affair. If it hadn't been for the release it gave both of my parents, we'd never set foot in it," Miller remembered.[12] Sports activities were an important part of the Club's offerings, with basketball, softball, and bowling teams organized for Club members. Defeating a hearing team was a cause for celebration. The Toledo Deaf Club still exists today, although at a different location on Adams Street.

Deaf Toledoans were also assisted by charitable and service organizations. The Quota Club of Toledo, a service organization of businesswomen, was founded in 1931. Its primary service project was to provide assistance and community-based services to hearing impaired and deaf individuals. Since its founding, the Toledo club has raised funds for hearing aids, batteries, and repairs; hearing screenings; TDDs for local hospitals; and scholarships for hearing impaired and deaf individuals.[13] The organization also awarded the Outstanding Deaf Woman of the Year, "given to a hearing impaired person in recognition of her personal achievements, community service, and who is an inspiration to other deaf people." The winner of the award locally went on to compete at the state and national level. In 1993, the Toledo club donated $4,000 to cover the costs to train a dog to assist a hearing-impaired individual.

Endnotes

1. Frances A. Koestler, *The Unseen Minority: A Social History of Blindness in the United States* (New York: D. McKay Co., 1976), 3.
2. Helen Keller, *The Story of My Life* (New York: Doubleday, Page, 1903). Keller's best-selling autobiography recounts her early years with her teacher, Anne Sullivan, and the way Sullivan taught her words using "water" as a teaching tool. Keller's life story was dramatized in the play *The Miracle Worker* in 1957, and a movie version starring Patty Duke and Ann Bancroft in 1962.
3. Twain is quoted in Georgett Leblanc's *The Girl Who Found the Blue Bird: A Visit to Helen Keller* (New York: Dodd, Mead, 1913), 14.
4. Keller's visit to Toledo was documented in scrapbooks about the Feilbach school located in the records of the Toledo Rotary Club, MSS-145, Box 14, Ward M. Canaday Center, the University of Toledo (hereafter referred to as WMCC).
5. For information on the history of the Lions Clubs International and Keller's appearance at its annual meeting in 1925, see http://www.lionsclubs.org/EN/about-lions/mission-and-history/index.php.
6. Article of Incorporation of the Toledo Society for the Blind, 1927, in the Sight Center of Toledo Records, MSS-179, Box 6, Folder 4, WMCC.
7. Article of Incorporation of the Toledo Society for the Blind.
8. Koestler, 147.
9. Koestler, 222.
10. For more information on the resistance of the deaf community to oralism, see Susan Burch's *Signs of Resistance: American Deaf Cultural History, 1900-1942* (New York: New York University Press, 2002).
11. The Education for All Handicapped Children Act, 1975 (Public Law 94-142).
12. R.H. Miller, *Deaf Hearing Boy: A Memoir* (Washington, D.C.: Gallaudet University Press, 2004), 46-47.
13. The programs and services provided by Toledo Quota are documented in the Quota International of Toledo Records, MSS-129, WMCC.

Helen Keller at the Feilbach School for Crippled Children in Toledo, 1925

Helen Keller and Alexander Graham Bell, 1902

Horatio Hubbell, the first superintendent of the Ohio School for the Deaf, 1827-1851

Thomas Whitaker and his guide dog Lord Byron, 1936

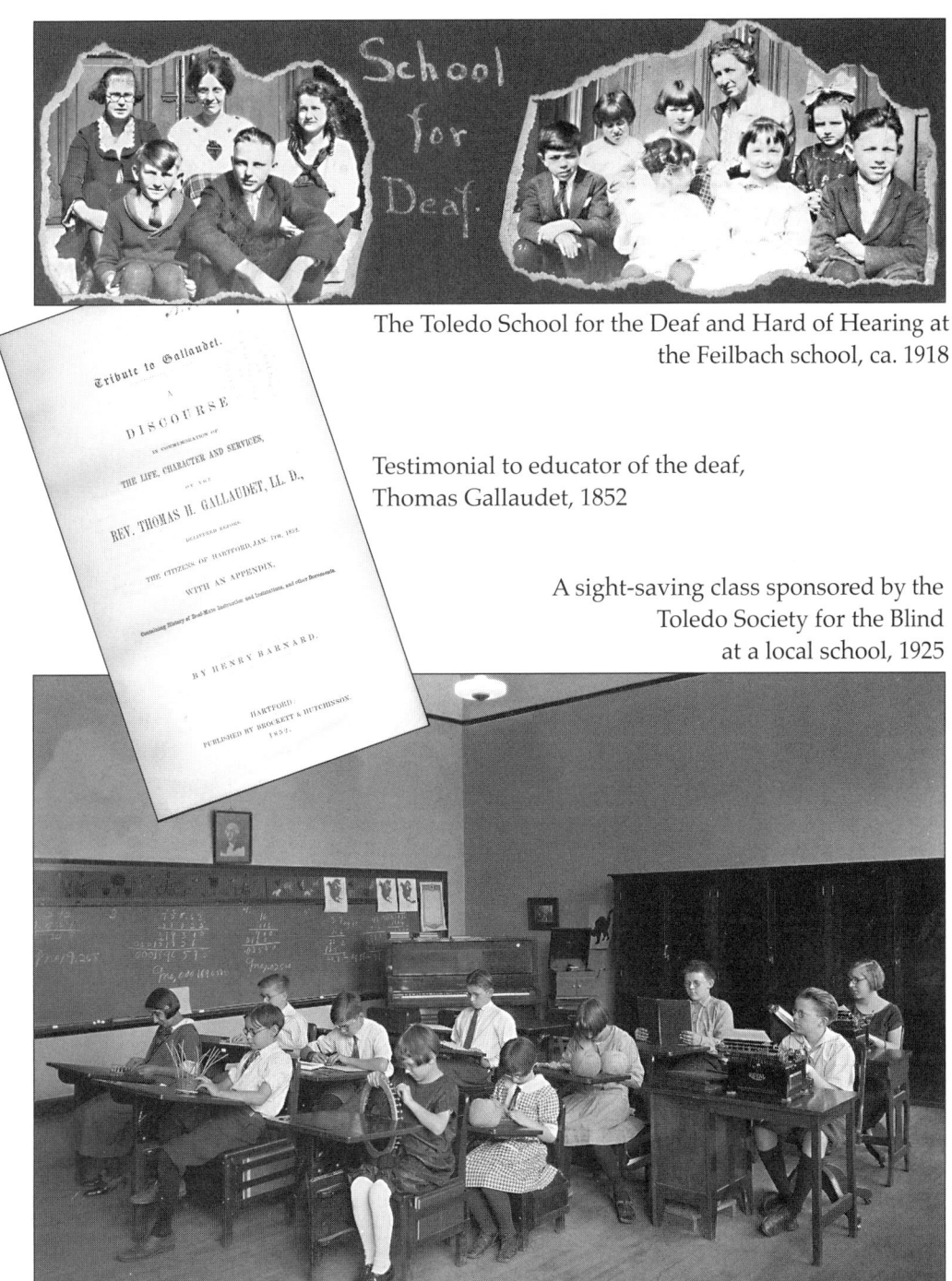

The Toledo School for the Deaf and Hard of Hearing at the Feilbach school, ca. 1918

Testimonial to educator of the deaf, Thomas Gallaudet, 1852

A sight-saving class sponsored by the Toledo Society for the Blind at a local school, 1925

George Beaudry demonstrating chair caning at the Toledo Society for the Blind during Hire the Handicapped week, ca. 1947

Toledo Society for the Blind workshop employees wrapping Jeep parts in paper liners for shipment overseas, ca. 1943

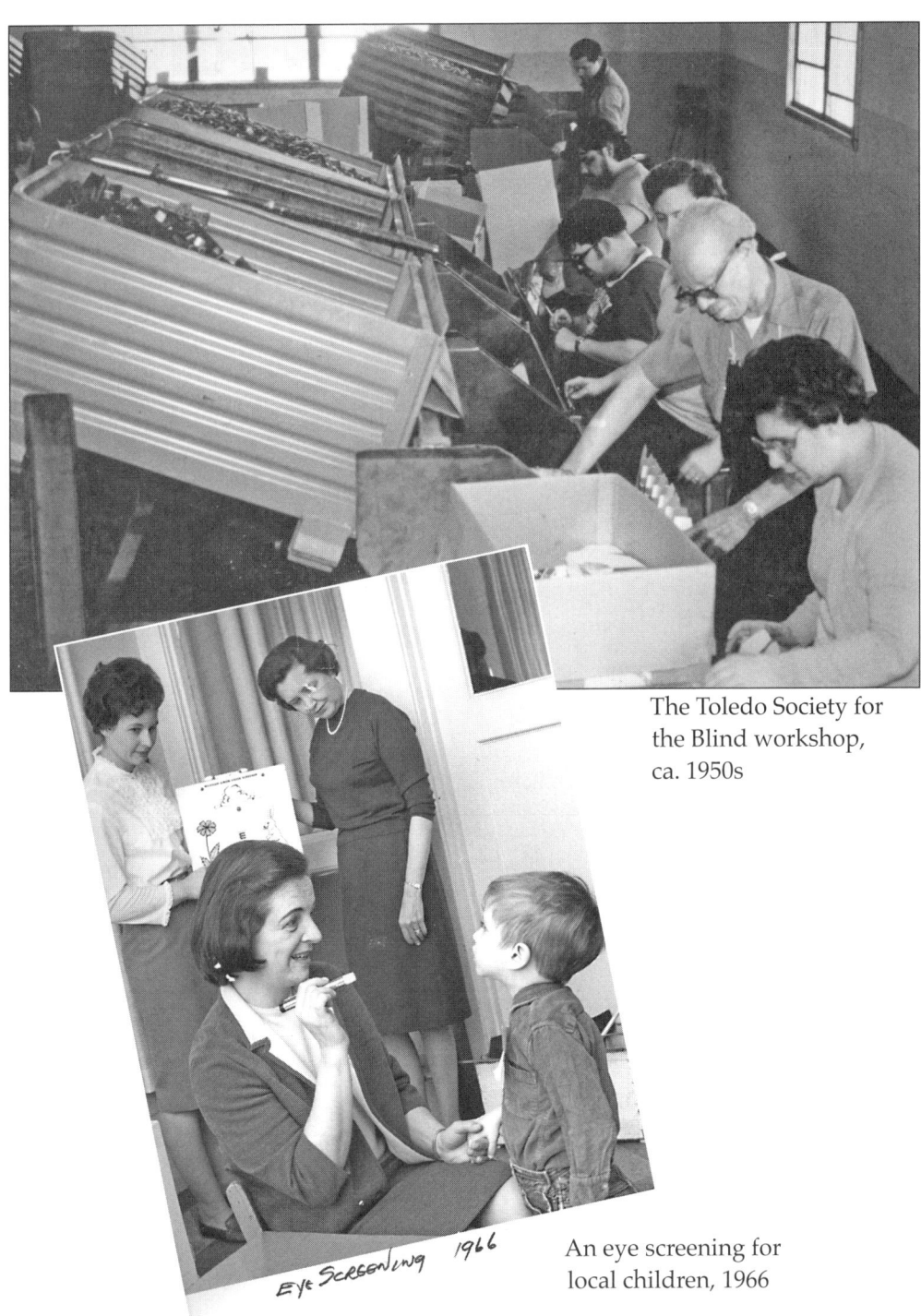

The Toledo Society for the Blind workshop, ca. 1950s

An eye screening for local children, 1966

Chapter 3

SOCIETY AND THE "CRIPPLE"
From Seclusion to Education

By Barbara L. Floyd

One day in the summer of 1917, a nurse from the District Nurse Association saw a boy in a small wagon. This fourteen year old lad, born without legs and without hands, had never been to school. After talking with him, the nurse asked what he would like best of anything, and he said, "To go to school."

From a history of the
Charles Feilbach School for Crippled Children,
published in the *Toledo Rotary Spoke* newsletter, 1946

The nineteenth century saw dramatic changes in the way those with physical disabilities were treated. For the first half of the century, those born disabled were mostly secluded in their homes as their families bore a social and moral stigma as a result of the disabilities. Fueled by the national belief that America was a country blessed by God and its people were his chosen ones, many saw those who did not live up to such expectations because of a physical disability as failures for their families and the country's future.

Many Americans believed that the improper behavior of the parents had caused children to be born with such deformities; too much alcohol, unsound minds, or "abnormal" sexual activity were blamed. Families with defective children were ashamed; keeping their children behind closed doors was a way to hide such secrets.

Of course, not all physical disabilities resulted from birth defects. Injuries, too, disabled thousands each year. With the American economy increasingly industrialized, dangerous working conditions in factories and industrial accidents maimed adults and children alike. Without a social safety net, such accidents had dire economic consequences for families who depended on the income of every member, even children, to survive. The Civil War left thousands of Americans with disabilities. Nineteenth-century technology also contributed to the carnage. The primary weapon of the Civil War was the .58 caliber Minié ball, a soft lead bullet shot with great force and velocity that flattened upon impact, ripping huge holes through bone and flesh. Immediate amputations were seen as the most effective way to save a soldier; an estimated 40,000 were conducted during the war. Mortality rates from amputations were high.

Those who did survive challenged American society's prevailing view of disabilities. Locking away the war's heroes like other persons with disabilities denied their valor and the country's sacrifice. Since veterans' injuries affected their ability to earn a living, the federal government provided pensions of up to $8 a month based upon the seriousness of their injury.[1] The war also fueled a prosthetics industry, as those with missing limbs had the right to be fitted with artificial replacements at the government's expense.

In the five years following the Civil War, the federal government spent more on veterans than it had in its previous eighty-year history. In June 1866, over 200,000 were given disability discharges. Thanks to improvements in treating war-related wounds, many disabled veterans lived comparatively long lives, with forty-three percent still receiving benefits ten years later. Finding work for these individuals was difficult; the government required that they be given preference for federal jobs because pensions only provided partial income. As they aged, disabled veterans were forced to petition for increases in benefits as their disabilities grew worse. Pension records detail sad stories of how many had to try to document their increasing debilitation. Typical among these was the pension application of John Broadbecke of Toledo.[2] Broadbecke's application, filed in 1875, described how, while serving in Tennessee, his limbs became swollen, and later he became deaf in his right ear. He was discharged from the military in 1864, and was "obtaining his sustenance from manual labor." He sought a military pension because his disabilities limited his ability to work.

The Progressive Movement Addresses Disability

In response to the struggles of disabled veterans, the exploitation of the working class, industrial accidents, and debilitating diseases like tuberculosis, social activists during the Progressive Era (the 1870s-1920s) sought to improve the conditions of the poor. Progressives pushed for social, economic, and governmental reforms. Believing that the environment determined individual behavior, Progressives thought by improving the environment, the lives of the underclass would improve. In the 1890s, many philanthropic organizations began to help the most vulnerable, including disabled persons. The Toledo Federation of Charities, the first local charitable organization, was founded in 1904. One entry from the organization's records dated November 4, 1904, read: "Young man, crippled right arm, called to sell stationary [sic]. Has an invalid wife."[3]

Progressives saw "crippledom" as a serious social and economic problem and believed disabled people could eliminate their dependency on society if they could be medically rehabilitated and academically educated. If successful, persons with disabilities could find jobs, as Progressives saw work as a fundamental right and responsibility of every member of society. Work itself could cure a person with disabilities, they believed, and finding employment could make a person's disability insignificant.

World War I further helped change Americans' perception of disability. Twentieth-century weaponry—particularly chemical weapons—produced hundreds of thousands of disabled veterans, despite the U.S.'s brief participation in the war. Some 930,000 veterans applied for disability benefits within five years after the end of the war.[4] Everyone knew someone who had been disabled, including a huge number who bore psychological rather than physical scars. The War Risk Insurance Act of 1917 set up a system by which veterans were paid a pension based upon the percentage of their disability. Advancements in medical care changed the way disabled people were treated by doctors. Using new tools like X-rays, orthopedic surgeons learned to "correct" disabled persons.

A goal of post-war reformers was to return the disabled veteran to a productive role in society. In his 1918 book *Reconstructing the Crippled Soldier,* Douglas McMurtrie stated: "Perhaps one of the greatest consequences for the future is the new attitude toward the war cripple—a human waste product at last being utilized. . . . For the cripple who is occupied is, in truth, not handicapped. America may have some physical cripples returned from the front, but she must have no social or economic cripples resulting from her participation in this war for justice and humanity."[5] "Curative" workshops were established to train the veteran in jobs where he might support his family and restore his self-respect. The Red Cross Institute for Crippled and Disabled Men in New York was the first specialized trade school and taught such skilled trades as welding, printing, and mechanical drawing.

Progressives also began to advocate for children with disabilities. Unlike nineteenth-century Victorians, Progressives believed children were not at fault for their conditions. The crippled child, if cared for from the earliest age, could become a model of improvement. He or she could be made self-reliant—no longer a drain on society or an embarrassment.

Joe F. Sullivan, who contracted polio at the age of four, was one such advocate. In 1914, he published a book, *The Unheard Cry,* a passionate argument for assisting people with disabilities, particularly children. The "unheard cry" was that of disabled people: "The cry of the Crippled has been drowned by the clamor of the other classes, and, as a result, the whole world, and especially America, is overflowing with an army of distorted, disabled, and incapacitated pilgrims, who, as a class, are recognized by the public in general as superfluous humanity."[6] He was particularly concerned about the need for educational opportunities for disabled children. "The public," Sullivan stated, "has agreed on the imperative needs of re-education for the crippled soldier in order that he may resume his economic place in life—but is apparently unawakened to the parallel problem presented by the crippled child, who is even more in need of tender care than the adult crippled."[7] The advocacy of people like Joe Sullivan impacted many progressive philanthropic groups. Stories about successfully rehabilitated disabled people—particularly children—began to appear in popular magazines. Between 1890 and 1924, seventy institutions were built nationwide for the care and rehabilitation of disabled children. Sullivan himself became educational director of a facility in Farmington, Michigan, called the Michigan Hospital School. It was in this capacity that Sullivan became the teacher of a severely disabled boy from Toledo named Alva Bunker.

The Toledo Rotary and the Crippled Children's Movement

Northwest Ohio played a key role in developing rehabilitation and medical services for disabled children through the work of the Rotary Club of Toledo. The national philanthropic organization of businessmen was created in Chicago in 1905, with the motto "Service Above Self." The Toledo Rotary was founded in 1912 and in 1914 began efforts to help the city's orphans, including several who were disabled. In 1915, member Harry Harper, a sales manager for Willys-Overland, suggested that the club endow a room at a local hospital where disabled children could receive care. The Rotary contacted the District Nurse Association and found that Toledo's disabled children were largely neglected. The club took a survey that year to determine how many children were in need of help. At a January 1916 meeting, the club officially took up the cause of disabled children, just as a major outbreak of polio hit the city. In the first year, 315 children were helped, many of whom were survivors of polio. The issue became a passion of Rotarians Charles Feilbach and Ed. Kelsey.

In 1917, the story of Alva Bunker, a young boy born with no hands and only one deformed, misplaced foot, came to the attention of the Toledo Rotary, although it is unclear exactly how. Some of the Rotary records indicate it was a nurse of the District Nurse Association who found him and promoted his cause. Other accounts say the members of the One Talent Club, a women's organization in north Toledo, sought help for the boy. Some reported his age as thirteen, others said he was sixteen. But the circumstances of his life are not in dispute—he was severely disabled. Without help, he faced a bleak future.

Alva Bunker's father was described as a drunkard and his mother overwhelmed by caring for the family. In 1921, Ed. Kelsey wrote, "We found Alva Bunker, that little boy without legs or arms, a mere stump of a lad, getting about by means of a roller skate on a board, just pushing himself around the alley. He was thirteen years of age, and had never been outside the alley in any distance. He had never been to school, nor downtown Toledo, or ridden in a street car or automobile. His whole world was encompassed by the dark grime of the alley. They said he was mentally deficient, too, and because so horribly crippled you shrank from him as you saw him, and he shrank from you because solitude and the surroundings of the alley made him afraid. You couldn't get him to smile because he never had anything to smile about."[8]

The Rotary Club of Toledo took on Alva's cause and sent him to the Van Leuvan Browne Hospital in Detroit (which had merged with the Michigan Child Welfare League that year to become the Michigan Hospital School) as no such facility existed in Toledo. Years later, a Rotary newsletter story recounted the trip. "The ride was a revelation to the boy. He stared, but did not talk or smile. He was turned over to the hospital with instructions to do the best they could for him."[9]

After several operations, Alva was fitted with artificial limbs and was able to attend school. Several Rotary members visited Alva three months after his surgery and found a remarkably different boy. While not yet fitted with artificial legs as he waited for the amputations to heal, he was sitting in a wheelchair, smiling, and sporting a gold medal for his studies. He had progressed to the fourth grade level academically and by the eighth month at the Michigan Hospital School, he had finished the eighth grade.

Joe Sullivan promoted the success of his pupil in many articles in the school's magazine, *The Hospital School Journal.* Alva Bunker was photographed building a rabbit hutch and with a sailboat he made. Sullivan boasted of Alva's improved outlook on life. "The cramped, embarrassed soul—conscious of his cruel deformity and illiteracy—is not the buoyant, hopeful soul of the other—conscious of his mental powers and possibilities and possessed of a new spirit of independence," Sullivan reported in 1920.[10] Alva Bunker's rehabilitation drew national attention from the articles that appeared about him. Joe Sullivan was compared to Anne Sullivan, teacher of Helen Keller, for his work rehabilitating Alva.

SOCIETY AND THE "CRIPPLE"

Alva Bunker returned to Toledo for a visit after receiving his artificial legs. He was driven by Rotary members to his family's home to see his mother. "She did not know the boy. He could walk upright, and looked like any other young man. When she heard his voice, she dropped a pan of potatoes, and caught him in her arms . . . the men who witnessed that scene cannot speak of it without having tears come to their eyes," the Rotary's national newsletter reported.[11]

The early reports of Alva's success inspired the Toledo Rotary to expand their work. In 1918, Emma Roberts, a nurse with the District Nurse Association, contacted Charles Feilbach, Rotary president, and asked him to help start a school for disabled children in the Toledo Public Schools system. Feilbach, working with school superintendent Dr. William B. Guitteau and Roberts, helped to establish the Crippled Children's School. It was housed in the old Central High School downtown (formerly the Toledo Manual Training School); the Rotary paid for transporting eight students to the school. The school soon grew to seventy-five students. After Charles Feilbach's death in 1924, the school was named in his honor.

Alva Bunker's legacy continued to inspire the Toledo Rotary to do more. As Ed. Kelsey stated in an address to Ohio Rotary clubs in 1921, "[Alva Bunker's transformation] showed us that all he needed was the sunshine and water of Rotary in order to make his soul blossom forth like a rose. It showed us that underneath the exterior, no matter how shrunken or how crippled the body, are wonderful possibilities if we put forth our time and talents to find them.… In Alva, we have received that inspiration that has gone around not only the state, but in Rotary the country over, until the work of the crippled in this state is becoming an inspiration of Rotary everywhere."[12]

Joe Sullivan pleaded for the work of the Toledo Rotary to go forward to other areas of the country. "May Alva come to realize more and more each succeeding year just how much good he can do in this life by 'keeping on keeping on' until his success will shine forth as a beckoning star to thousands of other sorely afflicted who may be less fortunate than he in the matter of being helped to help themselves. And may the example set in this case by the Toledo Rotary Club spread and spread until every Rotary club in the world takes up one challenge and hunts up at least one crippled child and see that it receives a chance that is a chance."[13]

The Crippled Children's Movement

And spread it did. In 1920, at a state-wide meeting of Ohio Rotary clubs held in Toledo, the clubs created a new organization called the Ohio Society for Crippled Children. In founding the state-wide organization, the Toledo Rotary collaborated with the Elyria Rotary, led by businessman Edgar Allen. Allen's interest in disabled children resulted from a street car accident in 1907. Allen's son died as a result of the crash because no hospital facilities existed in Elyria to treat him. Following the accident, Allen sold his business and devoted full time to raising money to build a hospital in Elyria. In the process, he found that there were over 200 physically disabled children in the city receiving no care. He turned his attention to funding the construction of the W.N. Gates Hospital for Sick, Crippled, and Deformed Children, which opened in 1919. Allen began to contact other Ohio Rotary clubs, asking for their help in assisting Ohio disabled children, an effort he dubbed the Crippled Children's Movement.

The purpose of the Ohio Society for Crippled Children was to "initiate, coordinate and direct the securing and compiling of information concerning the care and cure of crippled children."[14] The organization estimated there were 10,000 disabled Ohio children who needed care. All Ohio Rotary clubs were asked to join the Society; local clubs were encouraged to create their own local groups. The Toledo Society for Crippled Children was founded in 1920 as a chapter of the state organization. Sam Squire, former leader of the Ohio Rotary who had attended the Toledo meeting where the Ohio Society for Crippled Children was created, remarked that "crippled children all over the United States would some day learn to look back at Toledo as the place where was born an idea that brought them great benefit."[15]

The organization quickly moved from philanthropy on behalf of children with disabilities to advocacy. In May 1921, the Ohio Society for Crippled Children pushed for Senate Bill 174 and House Bill 200, which passed without a single dissenting vote. The new laws set up a system that became known nationally as the Ohio Plan. Parents who could not afford medical care for their disabled children could apply to county juvenile courts for help. After an assessment, the child would be sent for orthopedic treatment, paid for by taxpayers. Local school boards were required to provide education to disabled children. Rotary clubs assisted the effort by organizing clinics where families could bring their formerly secluded children to be examined by a public nurse to determine possible care and if the family qualified under the state plan.

On passage of the legislation, Edgar Allen said, "We have laid the foundation for the greatest piece of work for crippled children that has ever been undertaken by any state in the Union."[16]

In 1921, the forty-six Ohio Rotary clubs took the cause of disabled children to their national convention and that year, the Rotarians voted to create the National Society for Crippled Children. Edgar Allen was elected president; Ed. Kelsey, Burt Chollett, and Charles Feilbach of Toledo served on the board of managers. In 1922, representatives from Canada joined the organization as it changed its name to the International Society for Crippled Children, with headquarters at the Gates Hospital in Elyria. The international group was dedicated "to the service of the interests of crippled children throughout the world, to repair the tragedies of human nature and accidents which are registered on the bodies of little children, and to see that the bent are straightened, the broken are repaired, the weak are strengthened, and all educated."[17] Today, Rotary International continues this effort by working to eradicate polio worldwide.

The Charles Feilbach School for Crippled Children

The Charles Feilbach School continued to rely on the Rotary Club of Toledo for financial support. Nearly $1,000 a month was donated by the Rotary to the school, according to 1920s Rotary reports. The Rotary sponsored a Christmas party each year, helped to pay the salary of principal Nackie Wright (principal from 1918 to 1946), and provided clothing and essentials like toothbrushes to the students. Some Rotary members made the school a personal project, including Will Standart, one of the founders of the Standart-Simmons Hardware Store. He visited the school every day and gave each student a gift of a silver pencil on his or her birthday.

In 1930, the Toledo Board of Education approved building a new Feilbach School, constructed the following year on the corner of Stanley Court and Wilson Place. Pupils participated in many of the same extracurricular activities as other school children—planting trees, putting on school plays and Christmas pageants, and going on field trips and picnics, often with the help of Rotary members. Boy Scout and Girl Scout troops were established at the school. A newspaper article from 1933 told the story of two male students, one without a right leg and the other without a left leg, who shared a pair of shoes each year for eight years until they were fitted with artificial limbs. The students also sent birthday messages to

President Franklin Roosevelt and collected money to support Roosevelt's polio rehabilitation center in Warm Springs, Georgia.

In 1975, Congress passed the Education for All Handicapped Children Act. The new Feilbach school opened the following year on Glendale Avenue in south Toledo, with disabled students now integrated into the rest of the school population. Glendale-Feilbach School was built to be fully accessible to disabled children.

Rotary Continues Work on Behalf of Disabled Children

The work of the International Society for Crippled Children continued under the direction of Edgar Allen in Elyria. In 1931, the group passed its boldest statement yet on behalf of children with disabilities. The Crippled Child's Bill of Rights stated what the organization saw as the basic principles that should guide society's treatment of disabled children.[18] The statement ended with a sweeping call: "In brief, not only for its sake, but for the benefit of Society as a whole, every crippled child has the right to the best body which modern science can help it secure; the best mind which modern education can provide; the best training which vocational guidance can give; the best position in life which his physical condition, perfected as best it may be, will permit; and the best opportunity for spiritual development which its environment affords."

In 1934, the International Society for Crippled Children began a fundraising project to sell Easter Seals. The Easter theme was selected because the resurrection of Jesus seemed a fitting symbol for an effort aimed at resurrecting disabled children. The group renamed itself the National Easter Seal Society in 1967.

Alva Bunker

Little is known about Alva Bunker's life as an adult. Few Toledo relatives who knew him survive. His great-nephew, Charles Bunker, recalled some stories, part of the family's folklore.[19] According to Charles, Alva lived with his parents until they died and then was cared for by his sister. He could not find steady employment, so he supported himself as a chauffer and automobile mechanic working out of his home. He liked to read. He never married. There is one surviving letter from Alva written to then-Rotary president Gustavus Ohlinger in 1930 (when Alva was twenty-nine or thirty years of age), noting the continuing difficulties he faced trying to support himself. He again thanked the Rotary for "fixing my limbs."[20] But he also asked for assistance in finding work during the

SOCIETY AND THE "CRIPPLE"

Depression. "If you know of some one that needs somebody to drive a car, or do some small jobs, I wish you would let me know," he pleaded.

Alva Bunker died on January 2, 1979, at the age of seventy-nine. His seven-line obituary contained no mention of services; burial was private. The obituary left unsaid how he had inspired others to work to improve the lives of thousands of disabled children around the world.

Endnotes

1. For an extensive examination of how the federal government assisted Civil War veterans, see Robert I. Goler and Michael G. Rhode, "From Individual Trauma to National Policy: Tracking the Use of Civil War Veteran Medical Records," in *Disabled Veterans in History*, David A. Gerber, ed. (Ann Arbor, Michigan: University of Michigan Press, 2000), 163-184.
2. Buchanan and MacGahan Law Firm, Military Pension Applications, 1875-1889, MSS-046, WMCC.
3. Daily Report, Toledo Federation of Charities, 1904-1905. Family Service of Northwest Ohio Records, Box 3, Folder 7, MSS-075, WMCC.
4. K. Walter Hickel, "Medicine, Bureaucracy, and Social Welfare: The Policies of Disability Compensation for American Veterans of World War I," in *The New Disability History: American Perspectives* (New York: New York University Press, 2001), 238.
5. Douglas C. McMurtie, *Reconstructing the Crippled Soldier* (New York: Red Cross Institute for Crippled and Disabled Men, 1918), 40.
6. Joe F. Sullivan, *The Unheard Cry* (Nashville, Tennessee: Smith & Lamar, 1914), 15.
7. Joe F. Sullivan, Letter to the Editor of the *Detroit News*, "States Should Do More for Crippled Children," 6 January 1919.
8. Ed. R. Kelsey, "Crippled Children Movement in Ohio: An Address Before the State Conference of Rotarians in Cleveland March 21-22, 1921," as printed in *The Hospital School Journal*, IX (August-September 1921), 7-12.
9. Albert Sidney Gregg, "The Crippled Children's Movement and Personal Touch," *The Rotarian*, 22 October 1922, 181-182.
10. Joe F. Sullivan, "The Recreation of Alva Bunker," *The Hospital School Journal*, VIII (July-August 1920), 7.
11. "What Others Say About Alva Bunker," *The Hospital School Journal*, VII (November-December 1918), 11.
12. Gregg, 182.
13. Kelsey, "Crippled Children Movement in Ohio," 12.
14. Sullivan, "The Recreation of Alva Bunker," 14.
15. Resolution of the Ohio Rotary Clubs, 1920, in the Toledo Rotary Club Records, MSS-145, Box 5, Folder 3, WMCC.
16. Former Rotary Governor Sam Squire, "Use 'Ohio Way' for All Cripples," *Toledo Times*, 15 October 1921, 10.
17. Toledo Rotary Club Records, MSS-145, Box 5, Folder 3.
18. Bylaws of the International Society for Crippled Children, Toledo Rotary Club Records, MSS-145, Box 5, Folder 3.
19. "Crippled Child's Bill of Rights," 1931, Toledo Rotary Club Records, MSS-145, Box 5, Folder 3.
20. Charles A. Bunker, interview by author, Toledo, Ohio, 15 January 2009.
21. Alva Bunker to Gustavus Ohlinger, 18 March 1930, Toledo Rotary Club Records, MSS-145, Box 4, Folder 34.

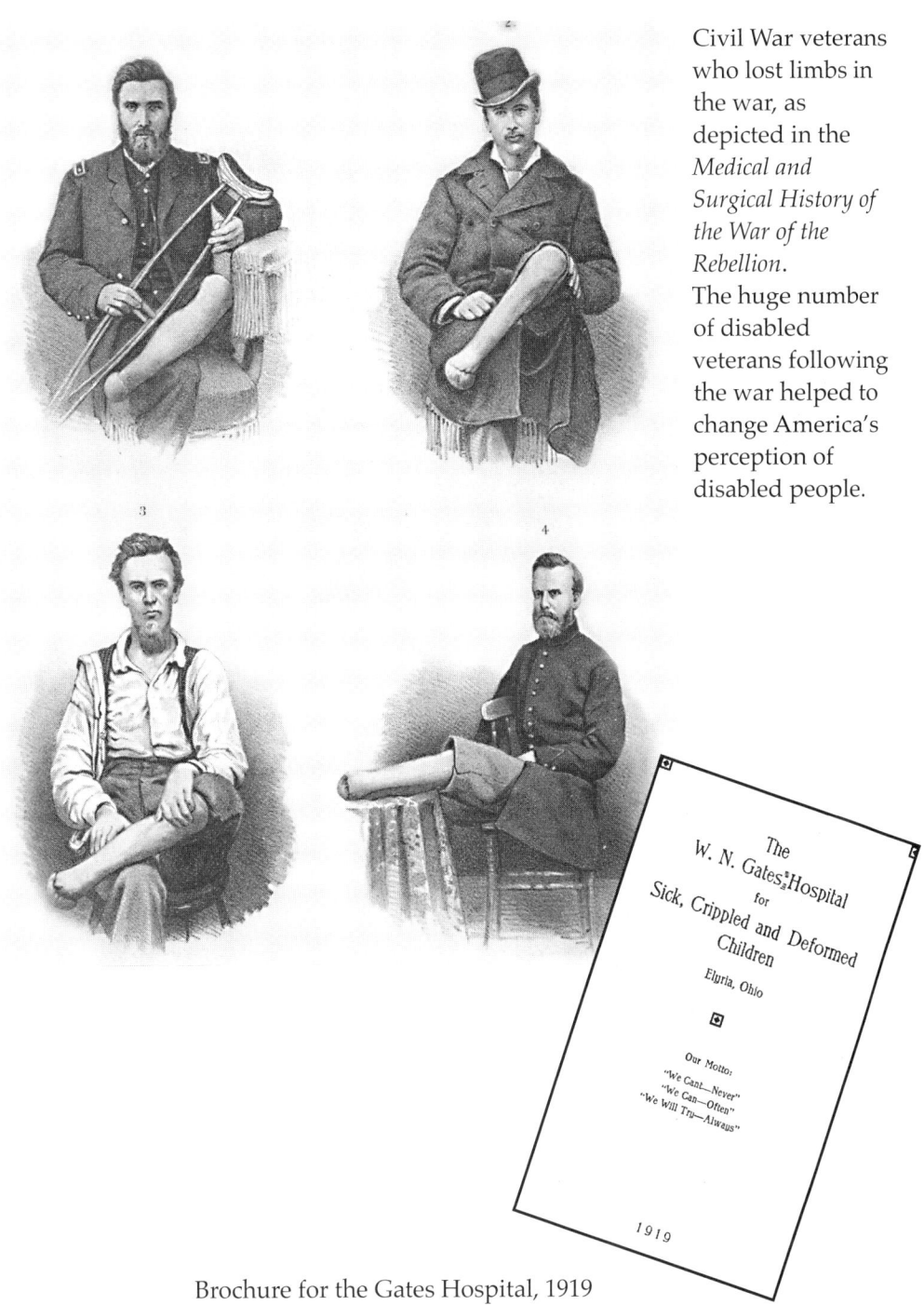

Civil War veterans who lost limbs in the war, as depicted in the *Medical and Surgical History of the War of the Rebellion*. The huge number of disabled veterans following the war helped to change America's perception of disabled people.

Brochure for the Gates Hospital, 1919

Alva Bunker, ca. 1921

Alva Bunker, the boy helped by the Toledo Rotary, ca. 1917

Edgar "Daddy" Allen, who started the Rotary's "Crippled Children's Movement"

Feilbach School students receive stockings at Christmas, ca. 1931

Rotary International made disabled children one of its major philanthropic efforts due to the work of the Ohio Rotary clubs, including Toledo

The Boy Scout troop at Feilbach School, ca. 1930

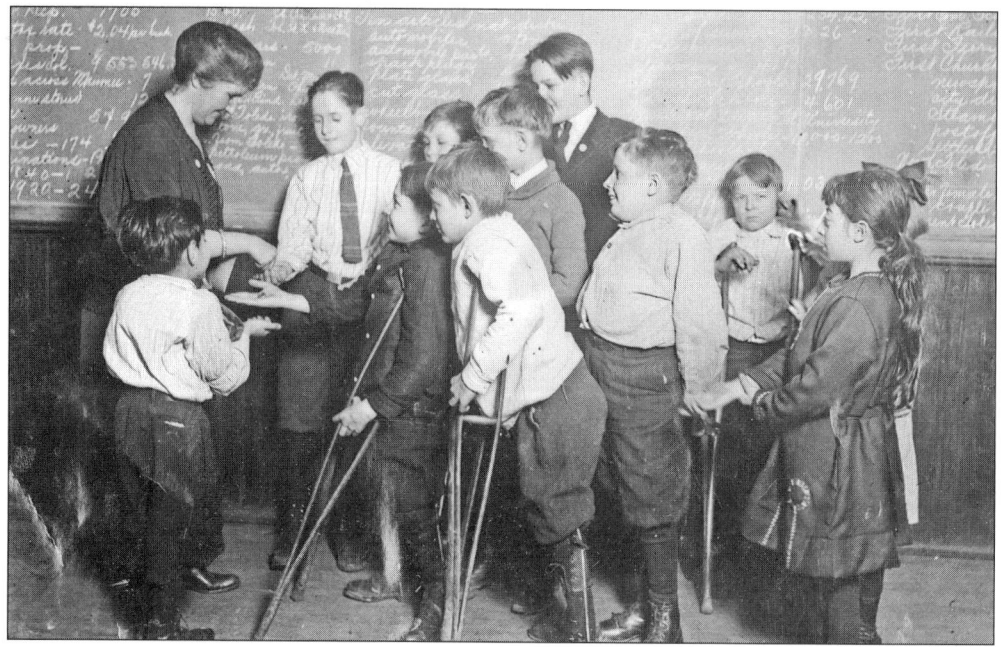
Principal Nackie Wright and children at the Feilbach School, ca. 1920

A dental hygiene class at the Feilbach School, ca. 1931

Students in a music class at the Feilbach School, ca. 1925

The notice of the death of Charles Feilbach appearing in the Toledo Rotary newsletter, 1924. After Feilbach's death, the Crippled Children's School was named for him

William Standart, who visited the Feilbach School every day

Chapter 4

CREATING THE "PERFECT" HUMAN

Eugenics and Disabled People

By Tamara Jones

The perpetuation of hereditary defect is infinitely worse than murder.

Scott Nearing, University of Toledo
Dean of the College of Arts and Sciences (1915-1917),
in his book *The Super Race*, 1912

Eugenics is the "science" of improving humans through a variety of methods, including selective breeding and sterilization. Supporters believed eugenics would increase the intelligence of humanity, conserve resources, and alleviate suffering. The term was first coined in 1883 by Sir Francis Galton, a cousin of Charles Darwin. Inspired by Darwin's work *On the Origin of Species*, Galton set out to see if evolution also applied to human ability. During the course of his studies, he observed that many of the British nobility had few children. To improve the species, he suggested that able-bodied couples should be encouraged to have more children. The notion of encouraging "fit" couples to have children came to be known as positive eugenics. Negative eugenics was defined as prohibiting "defectives" from having children. The eugenics movement continued well into the twentieth century and provided a justification to sterilize persons with disabilities and even to exterminate them.

Eugenics advocates used numerous techniques to decide who was fit to reproduce and who was not. One of the oldest was physiognomy and its close cousin, phrenology, both of which study an individual's physical traits to determine character and intelligence. Physiognomy was an ancient practice; its first known mention appears in a treatise attributed to Aristotle. Swiss pastor Johann Kaspar Lavater, whose popular works were first published in 1772, focused on the facial features to determine whether a person was inclined to intelligence, mental disorders, or criminality. Physiognomy featured prominently in the works of authors Charles Dickens, Charlotte Brontë, and Edgar Allen Poe; the movement's popularity peaked in the nineteenth century.

CREATING THE "PERFECT" HUMAN

German physician Franz Joseph Gall developed phrenology around 1800. Phrenology meant reading the bumps and fissures in the skull that were believed to determine a person's character. Both physiognomy and phrenology were often used to determine a person's intelligence. Not surprisingly, this often led scientists to associate certain facial and skull features with feeblemindedness, criminality, and other negative traits. Racist beliefs were also based on these "scientific" traits.

Survival of the Fittest as Social Policy: Social Darwinism

In 1859, Darwin published *On the Origin of Species* which described how organisms evolved. According to Darwin, those individuals with the characteristics best suited to their environment would pass these characteristics on to their offspring over many generations, while those individuals less suited would eventually die off. This "survival of the fittest" would result in an organism so changed, it could be considered a different species.

Unfortunately, Darwin's theory was twisted by the pseudoscience that came to be known as Social Darwinism. Despite bearing Darwin's name, the concepts were not his, but were based on the writings of Herbert Spencer and Thomas Malthus.

Spencer, a philosopher and political and sociological theorist, is perhaps best known for his support of eugenics and for coining the phrase "survival of the fittest."[1] He believed that human existence was full of struggles resulting in winners and losers. Any effort to interfere with this process was counterproductive. Spencer, therefore, opposed policies that would benefit the weaker members of society. This view was held by others, including birth-control advocate Margaret Sanger. To eugenics' supporters, humans improved through natural processes; governments and charities should not interfere. Those who were smart enough and strong enough would thrive and those who were not, would not. In short, Spencer's version of Social Darwinism allowed for nature to weed out the unfit.

Thomas Malthus, a political economist and demographer, promoted a theory of population growth used to justify sterilization. According to Malthus, a certain number of humans would always be relegated to poverty as the population expanded faster than available resources, especially the food supply, leading to starvation and other problems. In his *Essay on Population*, published in 1798, Malthus advocated both what he called "preventive" and "positive" checks on population growth.[2] Preventive checks consisted of moral restraint, vice, and birth control. Malthus defined vice as masturbation, homosexuality, and prostitution, while birth control consisted of coitus interruptus.

The upper class, Malthus believed, made effective use of moral restraint, but the poor did not, leaving them with birth control and vice. Those options, however, did not keep them from having too many children, which then led to Malthus' positive population checks—famine, disease, and war, which acted as natural population reducers. He believed that charity and other paternalistic methods of helping the poor had the opposite effect.[3] Because he also believed in the superiority of the upper classes, he worried that trying to help anyone else would divert resources from those who could advance civilization.

Although Darwin himself read these works, he dismissed many of the ideas as impractical or even morally wrong.[4] He thought of eugenics as evil and believed that all people should be treated sympathetically.

The Dark Side of Eugenics: Sterilization and Euthanasia

Eugenics quickly evolved from an intellectual exercise into applied reality in the early twentieth century. One well-known case was that of Baby Bollinger, born in Chicago in 1915 with numerous physical abnormalities. Harry Haiselden, a surgeon who delivered the boy, urged the baby's parents not to seek treatment even though some defects could have been surgically corrected. The parents agreed, and Baby Bollinger died five days later. It was later discovered that Haiselden had refused treatment to several other babies born with disabilities who also died. The Bollinger case received considerable media attention. Support for Haiselden was widespread and included such prominent individuals as civil rights lawyer Clarence Darrow and the editorial boards of some of the nation's largest newspapers.

In addition to the intense media coverage, the Bollinger case also inspired a movie, *The Black Stork*. In the film, a young couple wishes to marry, but is warned against doing so by their doctor (played by Haiselden himself) because the would-be husband had an unnamed "hereditary" disease that was passed on to him by his grandfather's elicit affair with an inappropriate woman. In an attempt to discourage the couple, the doctor shows them a variety of images of physically and mentally disabled people. They ignore his warning, marry, and have a child with severe deformities. Although the child's life can be saved with surgery, the doctor refuses, claiming it would be better for the baby to die. The film debuted in 1917, was re-released in 1927, and continued to play in theaters until the 1940s.

Letting disabled children die was not the only way eugenicists sought to "improve" society. In the first half of the twentieth century, they also used compulsory sterilization. The United States was the first country where compulsory sterilization laws were implemented. Indiana was the first state to do so in 1907, although Michigan (in 1897) and Pennsylvania (in 1905) had passed earlier laws but did not enforce them. In 1909, California and Washington followed suit. Thirty-three states would ultimately pass laws that targeted mentally ill persons, blind persons, deaf persons, people with epilepsy, and those with physical deformities. It is estimated that over 60,000 individuals in the United States were forcibly sterilized.[5] As late as 1956, twenty-seven of the then forty-eight states still had sterilization laws on the books, although not all were enforced. Support for forced sterilization began to wane after World War II, once the horrors inflicted on disabled people by German medical personnel were revealed.

Eugenics in Ohio

The eugenics movement's theories were also espoused by some who oversaw Ohio's institutions for people with disabilities. John Williams Jones, superintendent of the Ohio State School for the Deaf, discussed the need to control the disabled population in his book *The Greatest Problem of the Race—Its Own Conservation*, published in 1917 by the Ohio Board of Administrators, a state agency. In the book, Jones recounted the state's expenses for treating disabled people each year, noting that nothing was spent on studying the prevention of disabilities through birth. "Prompted by the enormity of the unnecessary sin, immorality, intemperance, self abuse, and the untold expense of maintaining and caring for the products of these undesirable things, and with the hope of eradicating much of them, and aiding the people to take a step forward toward better living, the Ohio Board of Administrators endeavors to put this book in the hands of all citizens," Jones declared.[6] The book included detailed charts showing how mental deficiencies were passed on through childbearing by "defectives."

While researching the book, Jones visited many of the state's institutions, reported on what he observed, and interviewed those in charge of the facilities. During a visit to the Ohio Institution for Feeble-Minded Youth, Jones asked how young people were kept from reproducing. The superintendent responded that a state law required such children be sent to the state home, and that the girls and the boys were "kept entirely from each other as well as from the public."[7]

Ohio had no laws requiring the mandatory sterilization of the disabled, even though the legislature considered such laws on several occasions. A 1904 state law did prohibit "the granting of marriage licenses to insane, epileptic and mentally defective persons,"[8] but it was rarely enforced. The annual report of the Ohio Hospital for Epileptics for 1909 noted that although the law was largely ignored, "it should receive the support of state officials, legislators, and all good citizens."[9]

Eugenics also had its followers in northwest Ohio. During his state facilities tours, Jones visited the Toledo State Hospital in 1917 and spoke with the superintendent, Dr. George R. Love. Love was quoted in Jones' book as stating, "The mentally enfeebled patients in our hospitals are the end products of sin,"[10] and that "these defectives should never have been born."[11] Love was particularly concerned about how to prevent mentally ill persons from reproducing. "One of the greatest problems facing the social workers of today is, How can we prevent the production of defective and neurotic human beings? Shall we go to the marriage courts, or shall we render the individuals incapable of reproducing his kind? At the present time, we are devoting our energies to the care of these people. This, of course, is right and proper, but it is not enough. We should find the cause and if possible remove it. Until we do this, we must continually face the expense of caring for larger and larger numbers."[12] He encouraged lawmakers to support "reasonable legal restraints" to prohibit disabled people from producing children.[13]

Scott Nearing, an economist who became dean of the College of Arts and Sciences at the University of Toledo in 1915, held many radical, progressive beliefs. He supported equal wages for women, the redistribution of wealth from the rich to the poor, and spoke out in opposition to World War I. But he also supported eugenics and wrote *The Super Race* in 1912. Nearing claimed that "the system of human mating must be perfected and the status of social institutions must be raised in order that the individuals produced in each generation may attain an additional increment of the qualities which will, in the end, produce the Super Race."[14]

There is some indication that Nearing's views of eugenics were tempered before his arrival in Toledo. In a 1916 speech on leadership before the Toledo Ad Club, Nearing stated that Americans once believed leaders had to be born from a select ruling class, but that this was changing. "Leaders are to be utilized wherever found. We look for efficiency rather than for nobility of birth; for service rather than respectable lineage; for education rather than eugenics."[15] Nearing was dismissed as dean in 1917, not because of his support for eugenics, but for his advocacy of socialism.

Oberlin College hosted the eugenicist William Kellicott Erskine in 1910 for a series of three lectures later published as a book. In the lectures, Erskine used statistics to support his belief that the intelligent classes were not producing enough children while the "undesirables" were over-producing. If this continued, Erskine saw immense problems for society. Quick action was needed if there was any hope of reversal. He cited Indiana's sterilization law as "commendable" and urged other states to enact similar legislation. In his Oberlin lectures, he also promoted the work of the Internationale Gessellschaft fur Rassen-Hygiene in Munich, Germany, which provided medical examinations of couples prior to marriage and passed judgment of whether they should be allowed to reproduce.

Eugenics in Hitler's Germany

The persecution of "undesirables" in Nazi Germany began with German eugenicists in the 1920s.[16] Post-World War I economic problems combined with attitudes held by many Germans fueled the rise of the Nazi party and the spread of eugenics. Inspired by the U.S. eugenics movement, German officials institutionalized disabled and other "inferior" people, forbade them to marry, and kept them from entering the country.

In 1933, only a few months after Adolf Hitler was elected chancellor the German government passed the Law for the Prevention of Offspring with Hereditary Diseases, which authorized the sterilization of anyone with the following disabilities: congenital feeblemindedness, schizophrenia, *folie circulaire* (manic-depressive psychosis), hereditary epilepsy, hereditary St. Vitus' dance (Huntington's Disease), hereditary blindness, or severe hereditary physical deformity. Those with such disabilities were targeted even if the disability in question was only moderate. Disabled children and infants were the first victims. By the end of the Nazi regime, between 375,000 and 400,000 disabled people were sterilized. In October 1935, the Law for the Protection of the Hereditary Health of the German Nation, which prohibited marriage between individuals with certain hereditary disabilities, was also enacted.

But sterilization alone could not achieve Hitler's goal of a healthy, pure German nation, so in 1939 the Nazis turned to euthanasia. They established six official killing centers scattered throughout the country that exterminated disabled adults. This "cleansing" program was known as T4, named for its headquarters at Tiergartenstrasse No. 4 in Berlin. Disabled Germans were starved to death, given lethal injections, or suffocated in gas chambers. After a patient was killed, the doctors were initially careful to fabricate a logical cause of death in order to avoid suspicion. If a patient's lungs were weak, the death certificate might list pneumonia as the cause of death. If the person suffered from appendicitis, the victim died of a ruptured appendix. The T4 killings were overseen by well-established medical personnel. In fact, doctors joined the Nazi party in greater numbers than any other professional group: by 1942, more than 38,000 doctors had joined, representing nearly half of all doctors in the country.

Of the six official killing centers, one of the most notorious was the Hadamar Psychiatric Institute, where psychiatrists ultimately killed more than 10,000 mentally ill Germans. Buses sent patients to Hadamar with such frequency that they became known as "murder boxes," and children would be warned against behaving oddly lest they "be sent to the baking oven in Hadamar."[17]

In 1941, Hitler officially put a stop to the killings because public opposition was growing louder. The killings continued in secret, however, and the program became known as "wild" euthanasia because it lacked coordination. Decisions about the criteria for euthanasia were made by physicians in direct contact with their patients instead of by a court set up for that purpose. Rather than gassing patients in the killing centers, officials allowed state hospitals to use starvation, drug overdose, or lethal injection. These killings were still being controlled from Berlin, but their secrecy meant that they were largely unnoticed—and therefore unopposed—by the public.

Beginning in 1943, Hadamar functioned primarily as a center for killing children. The "children's campaign," in which physically and mentally disabled youth were killed, continued even after the war ended.[18] It was not part of the T4 program, but like the latter, it started off small and unofficial but eventually became centralized and later dissolved into mass killings by local pediatricians.[19]

Although many doctors and nurses participated in the T4 program and the children's campaign, there were some who refused to cooperate by deliberately misdiagnosing their patients or re-labeling their condition as something which did not fit the euthanasia criteria. Others released patients to family members or hid them when transport buses made their rounds. Some doctors, such as Professor Gottfried Ewald, publically argued against the program. Although Ewald was a Nazi supporter, he was also disabled. Surprisingly, those who protested the programs were able to do so without losing their jobs, being reprimanded, or being sent to a concentration camp. As long as the protests were made within a medical context and not through public channels, there was no punishment or retribution.

The Aftermath of Nazi Eugenics

Even after Allied forces occupied Germany in 1945, the killings continued. The Allies had liberated the concentration camps, but had not yet investigated hospitals, asylums, sanatoriums, and orphanages. In August 1945, Robert E. Abrams, a public relations officer in the U.S. Army, was approached by a German physician who informed him that some doctors were still killing patients at the psychiatric hospital in Kaufbeuren. Abrams discovered that the accounts were true. A quarter of the patients had died, killed by lethal injection or through "scientific diets" (starvation). Over a hundred of those killed were children. At Eglfing-Haar, the U.S. Public Health and Security officers found the Kinderhaus, the children's building, with 150 young patients, including a "special department" where twenty children were being slowly starved to death. These incidents occurred after Germany had officially surrendered.

In 1946, Allied forces held war crime trials in Nuremberg. The first of these cases was officially known as *United States of America v. Karl Brandt, et al.*, but was known as the Medical Case because twenty of the twenty-three defendants were doctors. Some insisted that what they had done was not wrong because they were sparing disabled persons and their families unnecessary pain and hardship. In most cases, the doctors and nurses on trial insisted they were simply following orders given by the state. When the final verdict was handed down in 1947, three were sentenced to death.

Eugenics Today?

Although eugenics had largely fallen out of favor in the United States by the 1930s, forced sterilizations did not end on a large scale until the 1960s, and the practice continued until 1981. Today, many people with disabilities worry that some may choose not to have children, based on risk factors, and that people with disabilities could be further marginalized if society begins to select children based on appearance, intelligence, and the absence of birth defects.

Endnotes

1. Herbert Spencer first used the term "survival of the fittest" in his book *Principles of Biology* (1864). In this work, Spencer draws parallels between economic theories and Darwin's biological one.
2. Thomas Robert Malthus, *First Essay on Population*, 1798. Preventative checks are described in Chapter IV; positive checks are described in Chapter V.
3. In Chapter V, Malthus explains how, in his estimation, the poor laws of England did not help the poor but rather added to their distress by making it easier for them to marry and produce offspring, thus increasing the population without increasing the food supply to support it. "Hard as it may appear in individual circumstances, dependent poverty ought to be held disgraceful," Malthus stated. "The distresses which they [the poor] suffer from want of proper and sufficient food, from hard labour and unwholesome habitations, must operate as a constant check on incipient populations." Thomas R. Malthus, *First Essay on Population* (London: Macmillan, 1966), 99.
4. In *Descent of Man*, Darwin calls the instinct of sympathy "the noblest part of our nature," and stated his opinion that ceasing to assist those who need our help would endanger this instinct. "But if we were intentionally to neglect the weak and helpless, it could only be for a contingent benefit, with an overwhelming present evil. We must therefore bear the undoubtedly bad effects of the weak surviving and propagating their kind." Charles Darwin, *The Descent of Man and Selection in Relation to Sex* (New York: Appleton and Company, 1889), 134.
5. Hugh Gregory Gallagher cites this statistic in his book *By Trust Betrayed: Patients, Physicians, and the License to Kill in the Third Reich*. "Twenty years before the German Third Reich approved a sterilization law, the United States led the way among Western nations in the sterilization of the chronically disabled. Although the heyday of American sterilization came in the 1920s, sterilization procedures continued in some states throughout World War II and on into the 1950s. By 1958, over 60,000 American citizens had been sterilized." Hugh Gregory Gallagher, *By Trust Betrayed: Patients, Physicians, and the License to Kill in the Third Reich* (Arlington, VA: Vandamere Press, 1995), 52.
6. John Williams Jones, *The Greatest Problem of the Race—Its Own Conservation* (Mansfield, Ohio: Printed at the Ohio State Reformatory, 1917), 5.
7. Jones, 51.
8. *First Biennial Report Comprising the Eighteenth and Nineteenth Annual Reports of the Trustees and Officers of the Ohio Hospital for Epileptics at Gallipolis* (Columbus, Ohio: The Hospital, 1909), 28.
9. *First Biennial Report*, 28.
10. Jones, 135.
11. Jones, 135.
12. Jones, 134-135.
13. Jones, 135.
14. Scott Nearing, *The Super Race* (New York: B. W. Huebsch, 1912), 73-74.
15. "Nearing Wants New Leadership," *Toledo Blade*, February 1, 1916.
16. For more information on the euthanasia of disabled people during the Nazi regime, see Hugh Gregory Gallagher's *By Trust Betrayed: Patients, Physicians, and the License to Kill in the Third Reich*.
17. Alexander Mitscherlich, *The Death Doctors*, trans. James Cleugh (London, 1962), 21. As quoted by Gallagher in *By Trust Betrayed: Patients, Physicians, and the License to Kill in the Third Reich*, 7.
18. Gallagher describes how the U.S. Army troops liberating concentration camps discovered that, three months after the end of the war, the systematic killing of patients in hospitals, asylums, sanatoriums, and orphanages was continuing. Gallagher, 206-207.
19. Gallagher, 93-94.

Hugh Gallagher's book on the extermination of disabled people by the Nazis

Scott Nearing, author of *The Super Race*, 1912 and dean of the UT College of Arts and Sciences, 1915-17

A chart showing how breeding by "defectives" leads to feeble-mindedness and criminality, from *The Greatest Problem of the Race—Its Own Conservation*, 1917

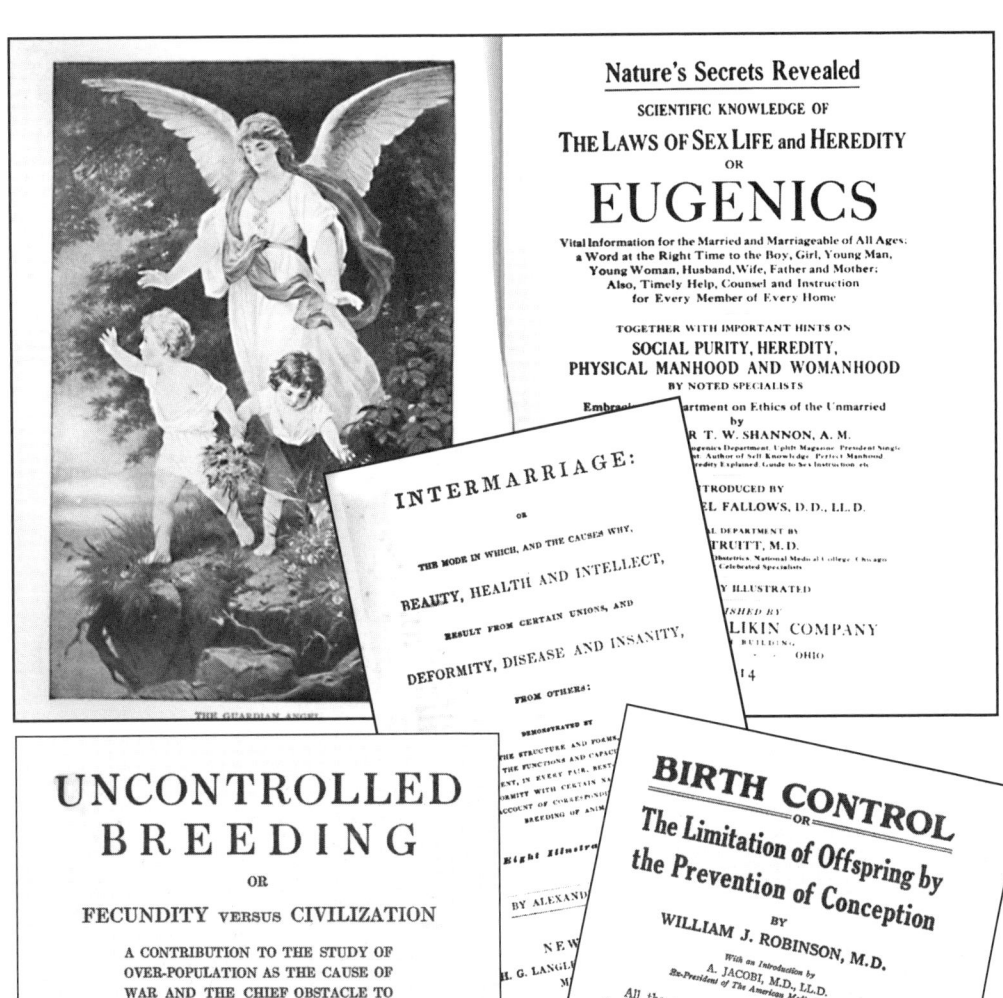

Some of the publications promoting eugenics from the early 20th century

Chapter 5

THE DISABLING DISEASE
Polio

By Barbara L. Floyd

Last May—a year after the onset of my polio—I was unable to care for myself in any way. During my 8 months [at Providence Hospital] I was taught physical independence. An ability to take care of oneself by oneself is one of the greatest gifts man has. Its loss is one of man's greatest tragedies.

Polio survivor Hugh Gregory Gallagher,
in his diary, 1954

Poliomyelitis is a viral infection spread by direct person-to-person contact, indirect contact with infectious saliva or feces, or contact with contaminated sewage or water. Symptoms are usually slight, if noticeable at all. It is only when the virus enters the brain stem and nervous system that it becomes a dreaded disease with long-term consequences. Polio destroys the ability of the nerves to control the body's muscles, resulting in paralysis, which can be permanent. In the most severe cases, it can immobilize the muscles that control breathing, causing death.

Commonly known as polio or infantile paralysis, the disease occurred regularly in the United States in the nineteenth and twentieth centuries. Polio generally affected children and adolescents, particularly those of the upper and middle classes and those living in rural areas who, it is believed, were not exposed to the disease in its less severe forms as poor, urban children were, and therefore did not develop immunities. The first recorded epidemic in the United States happened in Vermont in 1894. A severe epidemic in 1916 affected 27,000 people nationwide. Toledo experienced a major outbreak in 1935 at the height of the Great Depression.

But two outbreaks, in 1946 and 1952, defined the country's deep fear of the disease. In 1946, 25,000 people contracted polio, and in 1952, 58,000. The 1952 epidemic, the worst in the nation's history, permanently paralyzed 21,000 and killed 3,000. Between 1949 and 1952, the Toledo Contagious Disease Hospital treated 468 cases of polio in the city, with 33 deaths.[1] During the crisis, the polio ward at the hospital was greatly understaffed because volunteers afraid of contracting the disease stopped working. In 1953, another 250 cases were reported in Toledo.

Treatments for polio were few. The iron lung, a device invented in 1928, was used to keep alive those patients who could no longer breathe on their own. The machine was terrifying, both for those who experienced it and their loved ones who watched. The machine encased the patient's body from the neck down; a vacuum created within the machine forced air in and out of the lungs. Any breach in electrical supply could mean death. As awful as the iron lung was, it kept many alive and allowed muscles time to recover so that the patient might eventually be removed.

Many orthopedic surgeons believed the best way to treat paralyzed or weakened limbs was to immobilize the muscles and joints with splints and casts. In 1940, Sister Elizabeth Kenny arrived in the United States from Australia, touting an entirely different form of treatment. Although she claimed to be a nurse (hence the title "sister"), Kenny was not. She was, however, experienced in helping those who contracted polio in the Australian outback where she found that applying hot packs to limbs and gently exercising the muscles was far better than immobilization. Her treatment involved wool blankets cut into small strips to fit tiny arms and legs and boiled twice in hot water and then wrung out. The hot packs were applied to the limbs (but not the joints) and reapplied every two hours.

Kenny claimed remarkable "cures" using her technique, stating that she could restore movement in paralyzed arms and legs and make the afflicted walk again. She titled her popular autobiography *And They Shall Walk: The Life Story of Sister Elizabeth Kenny*.[2] Her self-promotion and battles against the medical establishment eventually led her to leave the United States on less-than-amicable terms. In 1941, however, the *Journal of the American Medical Association* released the results of a careful study of her method, agreeing that Kenny's hot packs were better than immobilization, although the method was not a "cure."[3]

The experience of Hugh Gregory Gallagher was typical of the ferocity with which polio struck. In the spring of 1952, Gallagher was nineteen years old and a vibrant and active student at Haverford College, outside Philadelphia. One day in May, he woke with a backache and stiff neck, and soon he was in intense pain. Gallagher found it difficult to walk to class and spent the next night at the infirmary as pain wracked his body. Within twenty-four hours, he could no longer walk. When his lungs began to fail, he was placed in an iron lung, where he stayed for six weeks. Within one week's time, Gallagher had gone from being a typical, vigorous college student to a patient on the verge of death. It was this swiftness of polio that made it such a feared disease.

While Gallagher eventually recovered enough to be removed from the iron lung, he was never able to walk again. He recorded his thoughts about the disease in a diary that he wrote in by attaching a pencil to his fingers with a rubber band.[4] While the diary covered only a brief period of his life, his insights about how his life had changed because of polio are riveting.

In 1954, Gallagher wrote about his first days with polio. "I am not sure how to describe the progression of unmovement. There is no sensation, no cessation, or on-start of pain. It is just something you sense is happening. You can watch it, or rather follow it, by flexing your muscles in the area of paralysis. Ah, you say, up to here, to here, and to here. To one who is aware of what is happening, as I was not, there must be a dreadful sense of finality about it. It is the silent ending of life in a living body."[5]

He sought to accept his permanent paralysis, but found it difficult. "What I am after is a genuine, real serenity of will and spirit. An ability to accept any happening or adversity with a calmness and a 'peace of mind.' I'm living through a pretty severe test of this now, but no worse a one than many others have lived through."[6] Eventually, the reality became more than he could cope with, and Gallagher suffered from deep depression which he later described in *Black Bird Fly Away: Disabled in an Able-Bodied World*.[7]

The Most Famous Polio Survivor

While thousands of Americans contracted polio, it was the plight of one person that eventually led to research for a vaccine. Franklin Delano Roosevelt was born in 1882 to a wealthy family in upstate New York. Through his family connections, he entered public service and in 1910, was elected to the New York Senate. President Woodrow Wilson appointed him assistant secretary of the Navy in 1914. Franklin was quickly following the same path that his cousin, Theodore, had blazed in becoming president of the United States. But in 1921, the thirty-nine-year-old Roosevelt contracted polio during a vacation at his summer home on Campobello Island. Sensitive to his position and his desire to have a career in politics, his family acknowledged that he had polio, but kept the press at a distance, stating that he was on the road to a complete recovery.

In 1924, Roosevelt traveled to Warm Springs, a resort in the middle of rural Georgia, where naturally heated spring water with high mineral content increased buoyancy. He was quickly impressed by his ability to move freely in the spring water and believed the exercises could restore his ability to walk again. He was so impressed that he bought the run-down resort for $200,000 (nearly two-thirds of his personal fortune) over the objections of his wife and mother. Thanks to a nationally distributed newspaper story, others polio survivors soon heard of the facility and began to flock to Warm Springs. Doctors and physical therapists were drawn there by Roosevelt; it became a major treatment center for those with polio. As the *New York Times* said in 1930, "the most beneficial feature of the resort was being able to talk to other people who had the same problems to meet and overcome."[8]

Despite access to the best treatments then available, Roosevelt was never able to walk again without assistance. The disease did not, however, stop his political career. Roosevelt learned to lock both legs in braces, and by leaning on the strong arm of his son, he could swing his legs from his hips, placing one in front of the other. By doing so, he could deceive many that his time at Warm Springs had indeed "cured" him—or at least that the polio had not incapacitated him. The press cooperated, and of the 35,000 photographs taken of Roosevelt after contracting polio, only two show him in a wheelchair.

Hugh Gallagher, who also sought treatment at Warm Springs, realized years later what most biographers of the president did not—that polio had been the defining experience in Roosevelt's life and impacted every aspect of it.[9] It was not a disease that he fought and beat, but rather something he struggled with every moment of every day. Gallagher called Roosevelt's ability to hide the severity of his polio his "splendid deception." Gallagher's analysis of polio's impact on FDR became the basis for his 1985 critically acclaimed book, *FDR's Splendid Deception*. Roosevelt died at Warm Springs on April 12, 1945.

A National March to End Polio

In 1938, to fund treatment at Warm Springs and throughout the country, President Roosevelt created the National Foundation for Infantile Paralysis. His friend Basil O'Connor was put in charge of fundraising. O'Connor organized national parties on the president's birthday that raised millions for the foundation. He also enlisted Hollywood celebrities like Eddie Cantor to raise money. The foundation became the largest voluntary health organization of all time, thanks to O'Connor's efforts.[10]

Most polio survivors could not afford Warm Springs and were treated at home. The foundation's local chapters became a means by which those with polio were identified and helped. Between 1938 and 1955, the National Infantile Paralysis Foundation spent $233 million on individual patient care.[11] While birthday parties in FDR's name continued to raise money, O'Connor realized that it was important to divorce the foundation from Roosevelt. He created the March of Dimes as a fundraising tool for the foundation. School children collected millions of dimes in their classrooms. Suburban housewives collected dimes in their neighborhoods to help fight the disease. As historian David Oshinsky stated in *Polio: An American Story,* "The portrait of mothers marching against polio became one of the indelible images of postwar America."[12] Between 1950 and 1955, the March of Dimes raised $250 million.

In 1950, eleven-year-old Susan Richards was sent to Warm Springs.[13] Born in Toledo, she contracted polio in 1941 when she was eighteen months old. Her father, general manager for WSPD radio, was frequently gone, and Susan was left in her mother's care. Her mother developed her own methods for treating her daughter's ailment that emphasized a sort of physical therapy. The family moved often, eventually settling in Washington, D.C. Susan could walk, but had an atrophied leg and a deformed foot which her doctor believed could be corrected at Warm Springs. For two years, she lived at Warm Springs with many other children, most of them with more serious conditions. She developed close friendships, and came of age at the facility. Her remembrances were collected in her book *Warm Springs: Traces of a Childhood at FDR's Polio Haven.*

Gallagher also found his time at Warm Springs to be one of relative happiness. "As it turned out, Warm Springs was the best thing that ever happened to me," he stated in his autobiography.[14] "Before Warm Springs, I had feared that I would be forced to lead the life of a lonely cripple. At Warm Springs, I found that I could have fun again. Just because I used a wheelchair did not mean I was unable to do things, go places, exert my personality, stretch my intelligence, or use my sex appeal." Gallagher also realized how important it was for both him and his family to get away from the demands of his care. "My going down to Warm Springs will give my family—especially my mother—a much needed but un-admitted rest. They have been really attentive and loyal. I must gain independence, for their sake as well as mine," Gallagher wrote in April 1953.[15]

While at Warm Springs, Gallagher had a chance to meet Eleanor Roosevelt during one of her visits. "Well she made a point of stopping, meeting me. She was gracious and interested and I was captured by her charm," Gallagher wrote to his family in 1953.[16] That year, Gallagher was co-editor of *The Wheelchair Review*, a bimonthly newsletter of the Warm Springs patients. The November 21, 1953, issue noted that two former patients were attending college at the University of Toledo.[17]

THE DISABLING DISEASE

The Race for a Vaccine

While continuing to fund individual patient care, the National Foundation for Infantile Paralysis turned its attention in the 1940s to finding a vaccine to protect against polio. The task was daunting. First, scientists would need to determine how many different types of polio virus existed. Then, a safe supply of each type of virus would have to be identified to maintain the research. Finally, in order to figure out how to stop the virus, the researchers would have to discover how the virus traveled through the body.

Between 1949 and 1951, three distinct types of viruses were discovered. Two dueling research laboratories fought to see which would be the first to develop a safe vaccine. In 1954, Jonas Salk won the race by developing a killed-virus vaccine that was successfully tried on 600,000 children. Even though the Salk vaccine was the first, Albert Sabin's live-virus vaccine, marketed in 1962, became the most widely accepted. While Sabin was the hero of the scientific community for his vaccine, Salk was the hero of the people for being the first to develop a way to end the dreaded disease.

In Toledo, getting access to the Salk vaccine in the first years of its existence proved difficult, and supply did not meet demand.[18] In 1955, Toledo received twenty percent of the Salk vaccine—some 12,000 doses—available in Ohio. To make the doses last longer, it was decided to delay booster shots in favor of giving as many as possible their first shot. A busload of first and second grade students from Birmingham School were the first to be vaccinated at the Health Department on April 22, 1955.

In 1962, the Academy of Medicine of Toledo and Lucas County and the Toledo Academy of Pharmacy started Project EPIC, "Eradicate Polio In the Community," the first mass immunization program in Toledo's history. Using the Sabin Type III oral vaccine, more than 300,000 children and adults were vaccinated that year, but not without some fear. Nationally, the Type III vaccine had resulted in a small number of polio cases. The Academy of Medicine questioned whether to go forward, but did so, switching to the Type II Sabin vaccine which it provided to over 900,000 people.

The Opportunity Home

When it came to caring for Toledo's young polio patients, once again the Rotary Club of Toledo and the Toledo Society for Crippled Children led the way. In 1925, the Society received $50,000 from the estate of glass company executive

Edward Drummond Libbey for the purpose of creating a convalescent hospital or home for disabled children in need of long-term care.[19] The Society established a committee to study the need for such a home and how it might operate. In 1930, the former Old Ladies' Home at Central Avenue and Collingwood Boulevard was leased for five years at the cost of $150 a month, serving as Toledo's first children's convalescent center. The Toledo Rotary agreed to pay $3,000 to cover the operating deficit for the home in its first year. Between 1931 and 1934, thirty-seven percent of the patients were polio survivors.

The Toledo Society for Crippled Children took a considerable risk in creating the convalescent center, which included a school for the children living there. Some members felt it would interfere with Feilbach School's success and that creating a convalescent home was better left to hospitals. "The establishment of such a home will not conflict in any way with the wonderful cooperation offered by various hospitals in the medical and surgical care of crippled children, nor detract from the educational work carried out by the Board of Education through the Charles Feilbach School for Crippled Children. It will, however, make more effective the treatment given at hospitals and will return to the schoolroom a stronger and more perfect body for education," Society minutes reassured in 1929.[20]

In May 1935, the Toledo Society for Crippled Children began discussing the possibility of constructing a new children's facility because the large number of polio cases were overwhelming the Old Ladies' Home. The Toledo Board of Education gave the Society land on Central Avenue. In 1937, the new facility was constructed for $300,000 and on its opening day in 1938, over 30,000 people toured the facility.

President George Shepard tried to allay fears for how the Society would pay for the new facility in his 1938 report. "May I point out, however, the Toledo Society for Crippled Children is a corporation not for profit and while the expenses must be kept within the range of sound operation, without extravagances or unwise expenditures of any kind, that in the last analysis—we will gauge our profit by the measuring rod of 'how many crippled kiddies did we help and did we do a good job?' "[21]

In 1939, the Crippled Children's Home was renamed the Opportunity Home at the suggestion of the Society's publicity committee. "It was the opinion that the name 'Opportunity Home' better expresses the opportunity we wish to exist for the children than any other name submitted," the directors noted in the Society's minutes.[22]

While the Opportunity Home provided long-term care to Toledo children stricken with polio, as early as 1950, the directors realized that a vaccine could wipe out the disease. Since the home specialized in the care of those with polio, the end of polio would necessitate a change in focus. On March 16 of that year, the president of the Toledo Society for Crippled Children authorized the board to articulate the requirements necessary for the Opportunity Home to become a full-fledged children's hospital that would treat all childhood aliments.[23] Before that change occurred, however, the Opportunity Home had to deal with the polio epidemic of 1952. That year, the home had its most rapid increase in patients in its history.

In 1955, with Salk's vaccine successfully tested, the Toledo Society for Crippled Children agreed to change the Opportunity Home's name and mission to the Children's Hospital of Toledo. The Society continued to operate the hospital. Within two years, the number of polio cases dropped to twenty-four, one of the lowest levels since the institution was created.

While it had changed its mission to move away from treating polio patients, the hospital still struggled to survive. In 1963, realizing it was no longer viable, the board of the Toledo Society for Crippled Children sold the hospital to the Diocese of Toledo. It became St. Anthony's Villa, an orphanage. With the hospital's sale, the Society returned to assisting children with disabilities. One concern was the lack of preschool programs for disabled children as Feilbach School had none. In 1965, the Society opened Opportunity Kindergarten in the former Edward Drummond Libbey mansion in Toledo's Old West End. That school operated until 1973, when Feilbach School began a preschool program and the Opportunity Kindergarten closed its doors. With its last facility closed, the Toledo Society for Crippled Children began to question the future direction of the organization itself.

Claiming Roosevelt's Legacy

While Franklin Delano Roosevelt's disability was not a public issue during his lifetime, the disability rights movement, begun in the 1970s and 1980s, saw Roosevelt as a powerful symbol. Some persons with disabilities faulted Roosevelt for hiding his disability, believing he could have used his experience to dramatically improve the public perception of disability. Others, such as Hugh Gregory Gallagher, believed Roosevelt could not have publicly promoted his disability during one of the country's most difficult times and still have been elected. The country was not ready for a disabled president.

In 1995, the issue of Roosevelt's disability returned to public attention when plans for his memorial in Washington, D.C., were revealed. The exhibit's sculptures did not show Roosevelt in a wheelchair. Hugh Gregory Gallagher and the National Organization on Disability led the fight to have the president presented as he was when alive. Those who opposed the wheelchair pointed out that Roosevelt went to great lengths to hide his disability, and would, therefore, not want his memorial to reflect what he tried to hide.[24] Gallagher, the scholar of Roosevelt's "splendid deception," did not agree. While Roosevelt never showed his disability, Gallagher believed FDR was not ashamed of it. Gallagher's argument eventually won when a statue of Roosevelt in his wheelchair was added to the memorial. In recognition of his advocacy to have Roosevelt realistically portrayed, following the dedication of the memorial, President Bill Clinton autographed his dedication speech and gave it to Gallagher.[25]

Endnotes

1. Barbara Floyd and Vicki Kroll, *The First 150 Years—A History of The Academy of Medicine of Toledo and Lucas County 1851-2001*, in collaboration with S. Amjad Hussain (Toledo, Ohio: Literary Circle of Toledo, 2001), 90.
2. Elizabeth Kenny, *And They Shall Walk Again: The Life of Sister Elizabeth Kenny*, in collaboration with Martha Osteno (New York: Dodd, Mead & Company, 1943).
3. As noted in Wallace H. Cole, John F. Pohl, and Miland Knapp, *The Kenny Method of Treatment for Infantile Paralysis* (New York: National Foundation for Infantile Paralysis, 1942), 5-6.
4. Diary of Hugh Gregory Gallagher, 1953. In the Hugh Gregory Gallagher Papers, MSS-185, Box 9, Folder 11, WMCC.
5. Gallagher diary, 1954.
6. Gallagher diary, 1954.
7. Hugh Gregory Gallagher, *Black Bird Fly Away: Disabled in an Able-Bodied World* (Arlington, Virginia: Vandamere Press, 1998).
8. *New York Times*, January 5, 1930.
9. Hugh Gregory Gallagher, *FDR's Splendid Deception: The Moving Story of Roosevelt's Massive Disability—and the Intense Efforts to Conceal It from the Public* (Arlington, Virginia: Vandamere Press, 1999).
10. David M. Oshinsky, *Polio: An American Story* (Oxford: Oxford University Press, 2005), 53.
11. Oshinsky, 65.
12. Oshinsky, 89.
13. For more information on Susan Richards Shreve's experience with polio and at Warm Springs, see her book *Warm Springs: Traces of a Childhood at FDR's Polio Haven* (Boston: Houghton Mifflin Co., 2007).
14. Gallagher, *Black Bird Fly Away*, 71.
15. Hugh Gregory Gallagher Papers, MSS-185, Box 15, Folder 5.
16. Letter from Gallagher to his parents, 1953. Hugh Gregory Gallagher Papers, MSS-185, Box 15, Folder 5.
17. *Wheelchair Review*, November 21, 1953. In the Hugh Gregory Gallagher Papers, Box 9, Folder 30.
18. Floyd and Kroll, 91.
19. For more information on the creation of the Opportunity Home, see the minutes of the Toledo Society for Crippled Children in the Ability Center of Toledo Records, MSS-190, WMCC.
20. Minutes of Toledo Society for Crippled Children, 1929.
21. Minutes of Toledo Society for Crippled Children, February 8, 1938.
22. Minutes of Toledo Society for Crippled Children, July 12, 1959.
23. Minutes of Toledo Society for Crippled Children, March 16, 1950.
24. For more information on the controversy surrounding the Roosevelt Memorial, see the Hugh Gregory Gallagher Papers, MSS-185, Box 8, Folder, 8.
25. Gallagher papers

President Franklin Roosevelt. Of the 35,000 photographs taken of Roosevelt as president, only two show him in a wheelchair

Postcard of the Opportunity Home on Central Avenue, ca. 1940

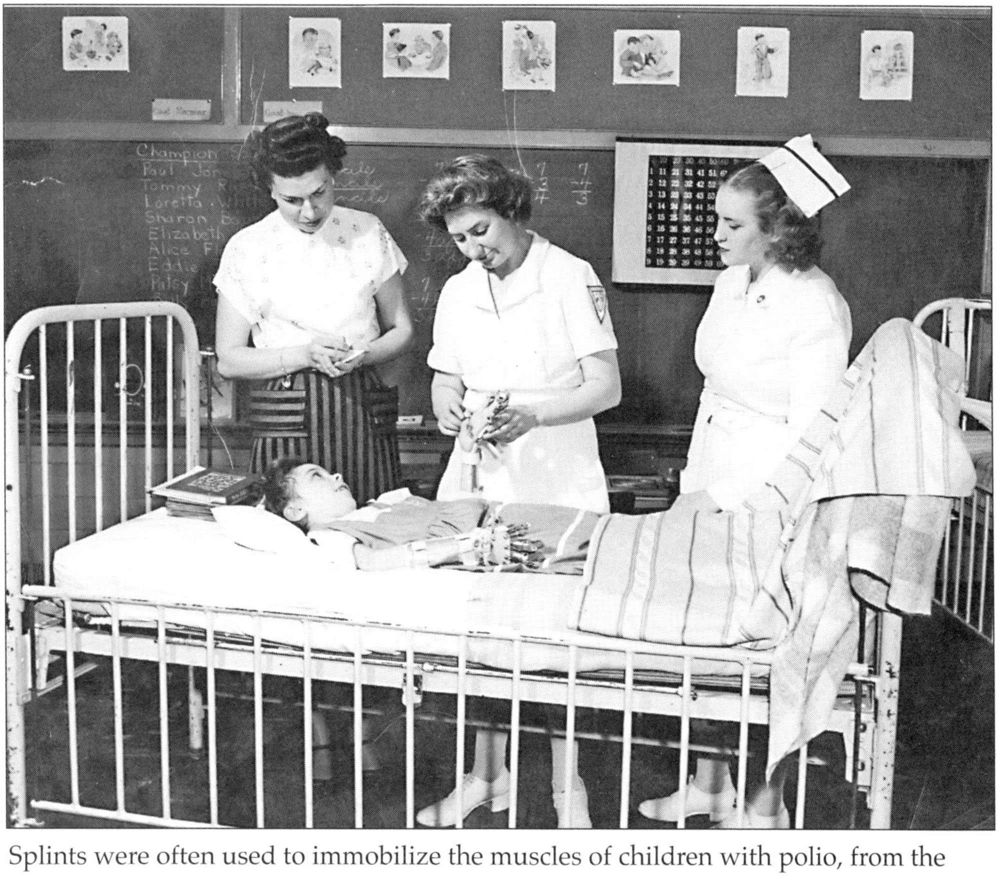

Splints were often used to immobilize the muscles of children with polio, from the Opportunity Home, ca. 1940

Sister Elizabeth Kenny, who advocated the use of hot packs for those with polio, 1944

Postcard of the Medical Building at Warm Springs, Georgia, ca. 1955

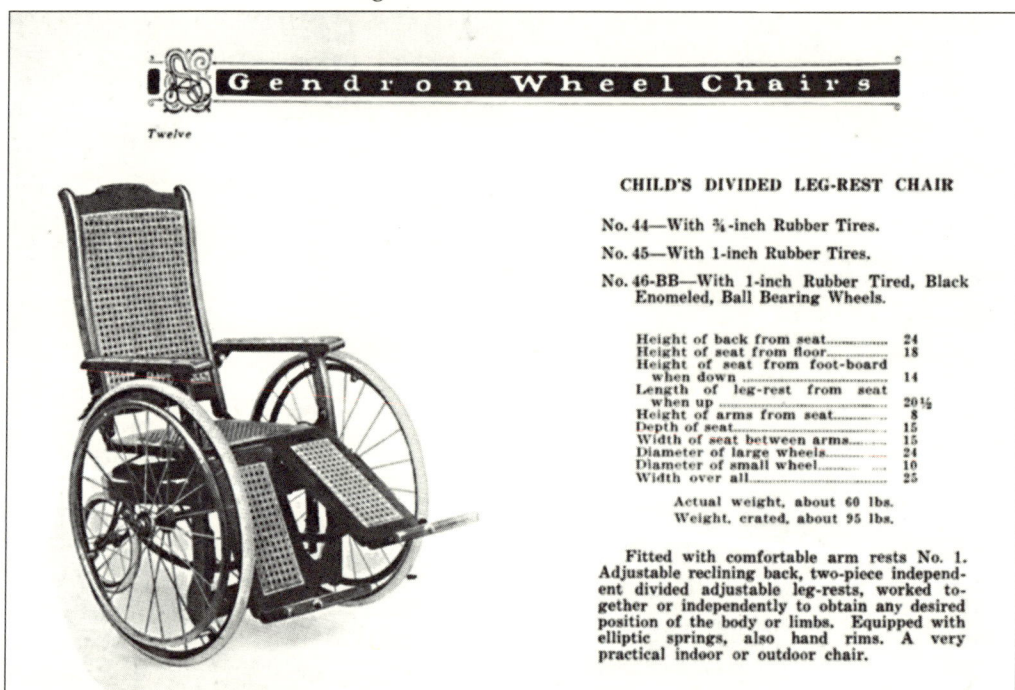

Advertisement for wheelchairs of the Gendron Company of Toledo, 1937. Due to the polio epidemic, the company sold many child-sized chairs

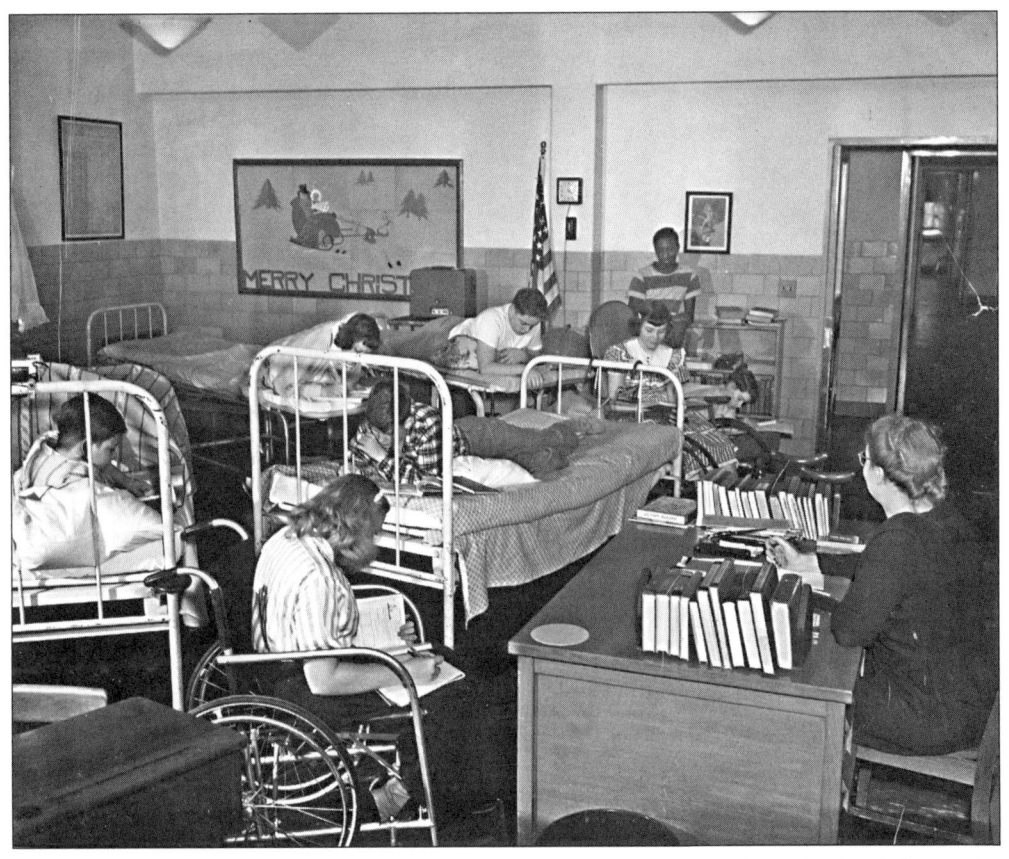
A classroom at the Opportunity Home included children in beds and wheelchairs due to polio, ca. 1940

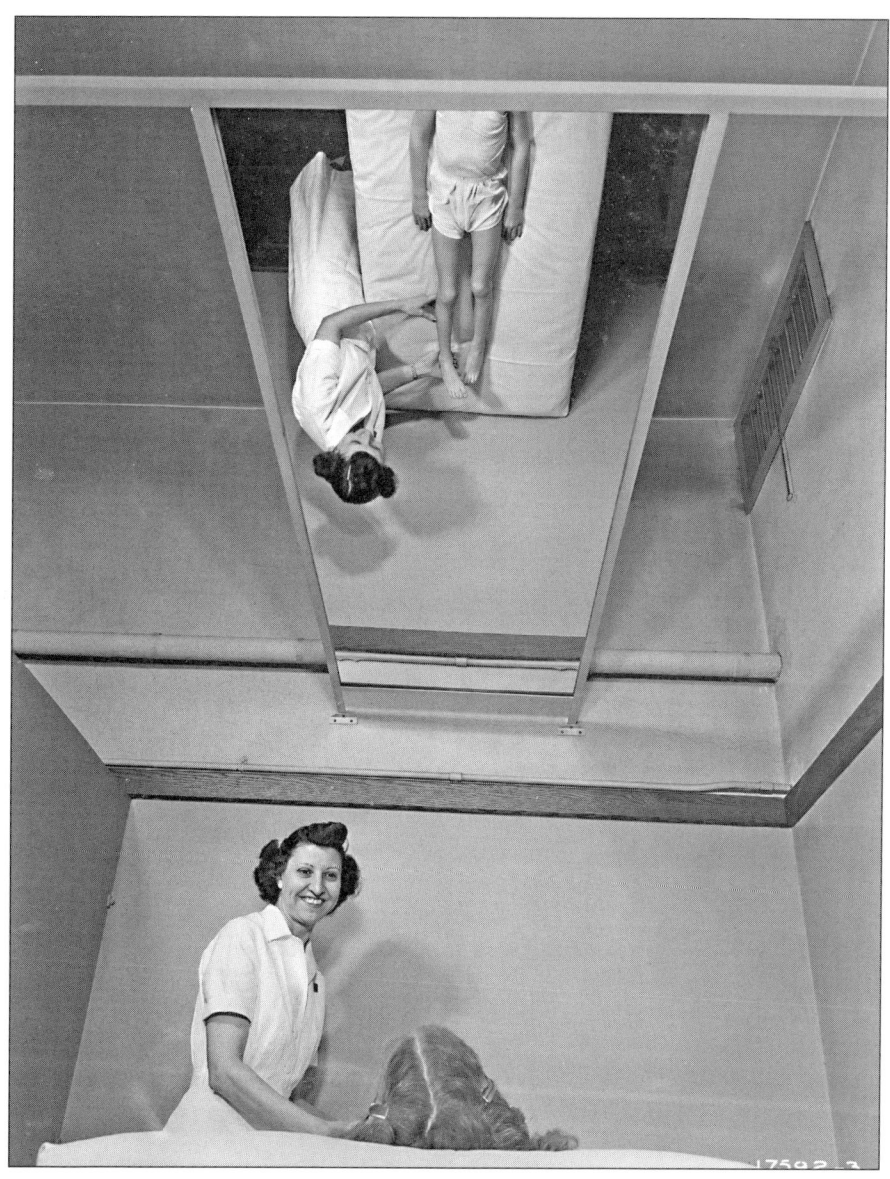

A nurse provides therapy to a child with polio at the Opportunity Home, ca. 1940

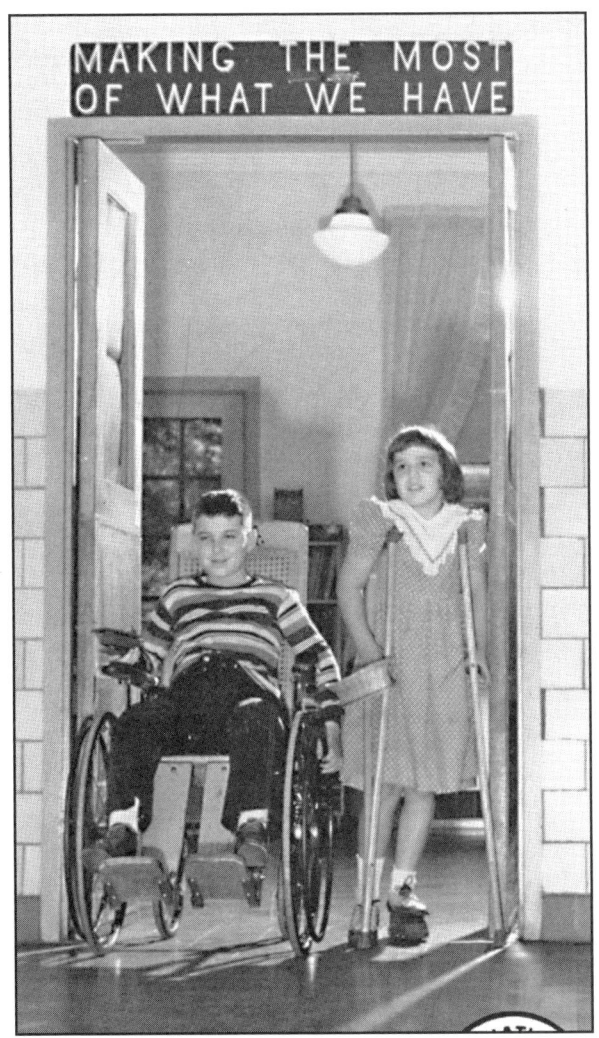

Children at the Opportunity Home, ca. 1950

A picnic at the Opportunity Home, ca. 1950

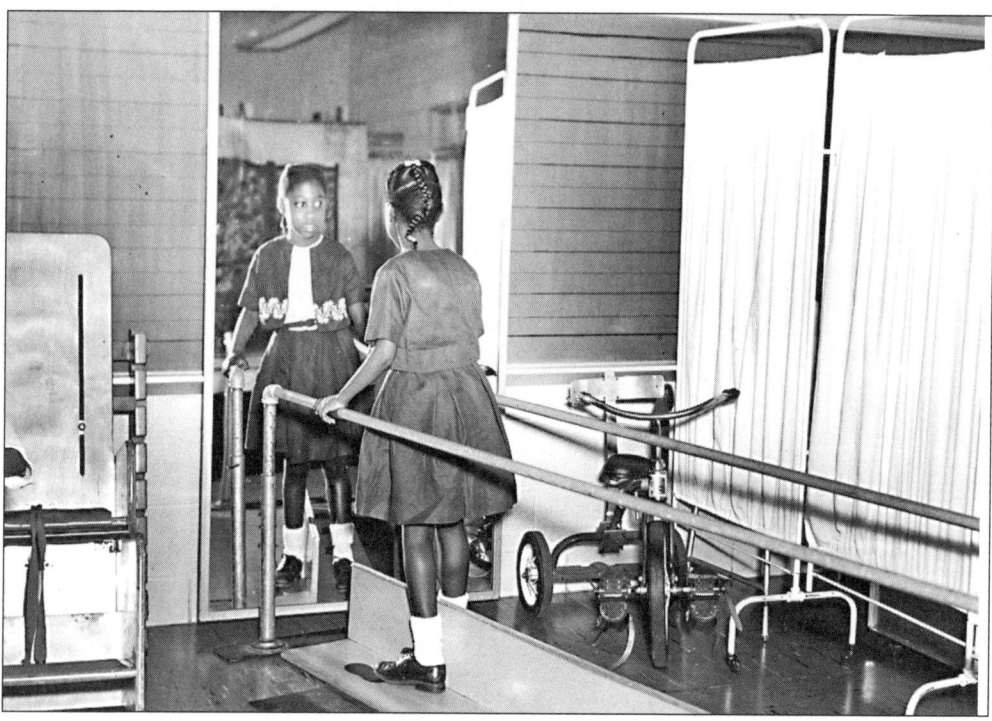
Learning to walk again after polio at the Opportunity Home, ca. 1950

Hugh Gallagher, who led the fight to have President Franklin Roosevelt portrayed in a wheelchair at the FDR Memorial, with First Lady Hillary Clinton before the dedication ceremony, 1997

Chapter 6

CUSTODIAL INSTITUTIONS TO COMMUNITY CARE
Assisting Developmentally Disabled Persons

By David G. Chelminski

Idiots and imbeciles as a group, though presenting certain characteristic peculiarities, properly belong to the great generic class of insane persons, the mentally deranged, and the mentally infirm; and though idiocy is, for the most part congenital, it properly includes a large number of persons who are feeble-minded from the effects of disease occurring in infancy and early childhood, before the age at which mental development is usually seen.

R. J. Patterson, superintendent,
Ohio State Asylum for the Education of
Idiotic and Imbecile Youth, 1861

The way in which American society has treated people with developmental disabilities has come full circle. In the colonial era, they were cared for by their families in their communities and were generally not an object of scorn or fear like those who were mentally ill. Rather, a developmentally disabled person was seen as the "village idiot."[1] They were idealized as children of nature, pure in their innocence and possessing unique knowledge. This view would not last long. By the 1850s, Americans began to believe that the best way to treat such people was to institutionalize them, outside of their communities and away from others.

As with the care given blind and deaf people, the early institutions emphasized education. Those who sought to educate developmentally disabled persons were influenced by the theories of Edouard Seguin of France. Writing in the 1840s, Seguin promoted "physiological education," a theory that developmentally disabled people could be educated by exciting their will and training their senses.[2] Through this activation of will, people with developmental disabilities could become socialized. Seguin's writings convinced Dr. Samuel Gridley Howe (who later married Julia Ward Howe, author of the lyrics to "The Battle Hymn of the Republic") to admit three "mental deficients" into his Boston school for blind children. Howe did have some success educating the children. Like his friend Dorothea Dix, who campaigned for better treatment of the mentally ill, Howe also visited almshouses where developmentally disabled people were kept and found their treatment disturbing. Impressed by Howe's achievements and shocked by the conditions he described, the Massachusetts Legislature in 1848 appropriated $2,500 a year for three years to fund the Experimental School for Teaching and Training Idiotic Children. Howe was appointed superintendent of the school.

The early institutions focused on teaching vocational skills so that developmentally disabled persons could return to their homes and find employment, becoming self-sufficient. The goal was to keep feeble-minded youth from becoming feeble-minded adults. But many of the children were severely disabled, making vocational rehabilitation unsuccessful. Schools began to classify their residents into two groups: those who were trainable and those who were not. Long-term custodial care quickly became the norm, especially for those who could not learn skills to support themselves as adults.

At the turn of the twentieth century, the rapidly increasing institutional population was a growing concern. Eugenicists, who believed that mental retardation was an inherited characteristic, argued that housing children in such institutions helped to ensure that girls and boys were kept separate and would not reproduce. Many states (but not Ohio) enacted mandatory sterilization laws for developmentally disabled people to further control their population.

Institutionalization and life-long care continued as the generally accepted method for treating those with developmental disabilities until after World War II. At that time, several well-known celebrities publicly confessed their struggles in raising their developmentally disabled children. The first parental story was by Pearl S. Buck, who published *The Child Who Never Grew* in 1950. Buck wrote about her daughter, Carol, and the difficulties she had finding appropriate institutional care for her. Buck's words were aimed at other parents in similar circumstances. "Parents may find comfort, I say, in knowing that their children are not useless, but that their lives, limited as they are, are of great potential value to the human race," Buck wrote.[3] Buck's book signaled that there was no longer shame in having a developmentally disabled child.

Three years later, *Angel Unaware,* by Dale Evans, told the story of the only child of Evans and her husband, Roy Rogers.[4] The book was poignant, as it told the story of her "Mongoloid" daughter who died at two years from the perspective of the child in heaven. Evans was even blunter than Buck in her assessment of why society put developmentally disabled people in institutions—so that they would not have to be seen. Evans donated the book's royalties to a new national organization, the National Association for Retarded Children, whose membership consisted mostly of parents of developmentally disabled children.

Perhaps the most prominent family to deal with the issue of developmental disabilities was the Kennedy family. Rosemary Kennedy, sister of President John F. Kennedy, was born in 1918 and diagnosed as mildly retarded. As she matured, she became occasionally violent and difficult to control. The family followed their doctor's advice for a lobotomy (a surgical procedure where connections to and from the brain's prefrontal cortex are severed), performed on Rosemary when she was twenty-three. The result of the operation was devastating—her mild retardation became severe.

Because of Rosemary's experience, the Kennedy family became major financial supporters of efforts to assist developmentally disabled children. In 1962, the late Eunice Kennedy Shriver, Rosemary's sister, started a special camp for developmentally disabled children in Maryland. Over 300 camps modeled after Camp Shriver were founded. One of these was Camp Courageous in Lucas County, begun in 1963. The idea of a national athletic competition for people with developmental disabilities grew out of Shriver's camps. The Special Olympics, funded by the Joseph P. Kennedy Jr. Foundation, held its first competition in Chicago in 1968; today over 2.5 million developmentally disabled persons participate in a variety of sports.

By the late 1960s, demand by parents for better care for their children contributed to the decline of large state-run institutions. In addition, a series of high-profile journalistic exposés, beginning with the 1972 story of Willowbrook State School in Long Island, New York, revealed the poor-quality care provided by many state-supported institutions. As a result, the education and care of developmentally disabled children was returned to the local level, with public schools and non-profit organizations providing services. As better medical care has increased the life expectancies of the developmentally disabled, the question of how to care for these adults who outlive their parents has become an issue for those providing services.

The Ohio State Asylum for the Education of Idiotic and Imbecile Youth

On April 17, 1857, the state legislature established the Ohio State Asylum for the Education of Idiotic and Imbecile Youth. The institution opened with nine pupils in a rented building in Columbus. The school's superintendent made his case to the legislature by stating, "Nothing in human form, nothing in God's image, however imperfect and degraded, should be despised or neglected, and idiots, more than all else, need human sympathies and protection. They are part of us, in our households, and we may not even indulge the wish to ignore their presence, or banish them from our minds."[5]

After the first two years, the school averaged between forty and fifty pupils. Within the first thirty years, the institution grew to house over 600 children. Then in 1881, a fire destroyed the main buildings. Fortunately, the fire was controlled "without loss of life, or even injury, to any of the inmates, officers or employees."[6] But the fire added to the overcrowding, as only 100 children could be sent home. The rest were consolidated into the remaining buildings until new facilities could be occupied in 1884.

By 1900, the number of school residents reached 1,100. The school was the first to experiment with detached cottages that segregated higher-functioning children from those who were lower-functioning. Its stated mission remained education and was described to the Ohio legislature as providing education so each pupil could develop "such industrial power as they possess . . . in their own support."[7] Male students were trained in gardening and agriculture on a farm purchased by the school; females were taught domestic skills. But in 1900, new buildings were added that accommodated 400 of each sex who received only custodial care. Those in charge of the school also recognized "the duty of providing against the increase of this unfortunate class, by placing them under such restrictions as will prevent the multiplying of their kind."

The facility's name was changed to the Columbus State Institute for the Mentally Retarded in the early 1900s. By 1917, the Institute had over 2,400 residents, twice the number of ten years before. As with the state's mental health facilities, overcrowding led to poorer quality care. The Institute also continued to struggle with education versus custodial care. After parents in the 1950s began to advocate for better quality care, a state committee chaired by Dr. Raymond Horn was created in 1960 to examine how Ohio could improve its facilities. The committee's report recommended establishing a county system to oversee programs for developmentally disabled persons funded by local, state, and federal funds. That legislation was approved in 1967; the state school was replaced with county programs and educational facilities.

Josina Lott and the Developmentally Disabled Children of Toledo

In 1938, Josina Jones Lott moved with her husband and son from Michigan to Toledo's Old West End, where she was disturbed to find the public schools turning away children with developmental disabilities. That September, Lott began what she called her "experiment" to prove there are no "uneducable children" by starting a day school in her upstairs Whitney Avenue apartment.[8] She began teaching a basic first-grade curriculum to one girl who had cerebral palsy. By the end of the first year, the child had mastered skills in reading, writing, and arithmetic. One child became four children, and before long Lott had fifteen students.

Lott sought local educational opportunities instead of state institutional care for her students. In 1940, as more parents were asking Lott to teach their children, she moved her fifty students to the basement of Rosewood Presbyterian Church. She set up her educational program to conform to the Board of Education's academic standards, but also stressed speech, art, and music. Tuition was five dollars a week. In the days when developmentally disabled children were frequently kept out of sight because of the shame felt by parents, Lott recalled that she was lucky to have one parent attend the school's programs when invited to do so.

After receiving help from the Toledo Board of Education and the Chamber of Commerce, the Lott Day School, a not-for-profit corporation, was created in 1945 and moved to a building at Kelsey and Heffner streets. Seeing another unmet need, Lott later asked the school auxiliary for funds to open a sheltered workshop to employ students who had matured and reached their limits academically but could not find work as adults. In doing so, she created one of the first non-institutionalized programs in the nation that provided vocational training for developmentally disabled people. The goal of the workshop was to train young adults in skills that would allow them to become independent.

In 1950, the Lucas County Association for Retarded Children was created by parents as an advocate group for the county's developmentally disabled. These parents included Jay Shuer, who had attended the first convention of the National Association for Parents and Friends of Mentally Retarded Children that year. At the national convention, Alan Simpson, chair of the steering committee, noted the importance of the national gathering. "This is a thrilling and auspicious occasion; another milestone, carved from travail and tears, and indomitable purpose, in the progress against intolerance, for understanding."[9]

In 1955, Lott's sheltered workshop program—called the Sheltered Workshop Foundation of Toledo at first but later changed to Lott Industries—was incorporated, and located next to the Lott Day School. To pay for the building, the board members personally lent the organization $1,000 each.[10] In 1957, Lucas County taxpayers approved a levy to support the school and workshop, as the Lucas County Child Welfare Board took over financial control of the Lott Day School. With county support, services for developmentally disabled children expanded, including the opening of Tracy School in 1961 (later the Jay Shuer

School) in a former Toledo Public Schools building and the construction of the Larc Lane School a year later. Coordination of the many programs was turned over to a new organization, the Lucas County Board of Mental Retardation, in 1967. Josina Lott died in 1972 at the age of seventy-four.

In 1975, federal law changed, requiring all children to have access to public education. Children were moved from Larc Lane and Jay Shuer schools into the public school system, and as a result, the two schools closed. Lott Industries is now a private, not-for-profit corporation that serves about 1,200 people in Toledo, providing employment, therapy, and recreation.

In Wood County, programs for children with developmental disabilities were also an outgrowth of the parents' movement.[11] In 1955, the parents of twelve children met to discuss the need for a school in the county. Because of the largely rural nature of Wood County, serving developmentally disabled children was even more difficult than in urban Toledo. The first classes were held in 1956, in Ridge School in Bowling Green. The school moved several times until 1972, when the new Wood Lane School opened. Operated by the Wood County Board of Mental Retardation and Developmental Disabilities, the school continues to offer educational programs for developmentally disabled children, and operates Wood Lane Industries, a sheltered workshop for adults.

Decem Center and GOAL for the Profoundly Retarded

Another parents' organization, GOAL for the Profoundly Retarded, was created in the early 1970s for those with older children with profound developmental disabilities.[12] It began as a program where parents with home-bound developmentally disabled children and adult children could exchange equipment and services with other parents. The group also sought to establish physical therapy and parent relief programs, and provided peer support and advice. One of its leaders was Anne Grady, who had a severely disabled son. Grady found that as her son grew older, she was unable to continue to care for him, but there were few services available.

In 1972, GOAL established a temporary day care program at St. Andrews' Episcopal Church where parents could bring their children for the day, allowing them some free time and assisting those with jobs outside the home. In 1973, the center changed its name to the Lucas County Day Care Center, and moved to a building on Parkwood Avenue. Then-president John Bognar wrote a grant for the project, and it was funded by the state of Ohio.

Ten years later, in May 1982, the Decem Center was dedicated in a new building on Eber Road near Holland, Ohio, to provide long-term care for profoundly developmentally disabled adults. Decem was an independent group home for those who were leaving other facilities through the state's "deinstitutionalization" program. The Center was named Decem, the Latin word for ten, because it served ten counties in northwest Ohio. The Decem Center filled an important need for parents with adult developmentally disabled children, an area that was underserved by other social service agencies. The mission of the Decem Center was to provide a full, enriched life in the least restrictive environment possible for its clients. They refrained from the use of unnecessary physical and chemical restraints.

In the late 1980s, the Decem Center changed its name to the Anne Grady Center in honor of one of its founders. Today it is one of the homes of Anne Grady Services, which includes four other group homes; "Annie's House," a respite home for children who are medically fragile, and Prescribed Pediatric Center, a medical day care facility.

The mission of Anne Grady Services is to provide dignity, respect, and quality services to people with disabilities and their families, helping their clients to reach their highest potential. It serves 195 people from northwest Ohio.

Sunshine Children's Home

Another program for northwest Ohio's severely disabled children was started by Roy and Georgette Engler.[13] In 1931, when their twin daughters began school, the Englers were stunned when their teacher told them the children were developmentally disabled. Subsequent examination revealed that all five of their surviving children were also developmentally disabled. For the Englers, institutionalization was out of the question. Alternative services for their children were either substandard or nonexistent.

In 1949, Georgette Engler's mother gave her two-story frame house and seven acres of farmland on Maumee Western Road in Maumee. The Engler family moved into the house and a small single-story building was erected that would become the Sunshine Children's Home. The approach from the outset was "to provide loving care in a clean, home-like environment." Assisted by their own children, the Englers operated the home (licensed by the state in 1951) until 1952, when an advisory board was created to provide a more formal structure. Sunshine Children's Home was incorporated as a nonprofit organization "to provide care for Down syndrome [then referred to as Mongoloid], spastic, and mentally retarded children."[14]

With materials donated by local building suppliers, volunteer construction workers added a second story in 1952 for the Engler family's living quarters. This would be the first of several expansions built by volunteer construction-trades professionals. In 1954, the Englers attracted national attention for their unique home by appearing on the May 7 broadcast of the "Welcome Travelers" radio program. In September 1957, the *Maumee Valley News* reported that "a state building inspector, who recently paid a visit to Sunshine Children's Home, reported that after a thorough investigation that it was the only institution he had ever seen in which he could find no conditions to be improved."

In December 1959, women from the Central Mennonite Church in Archbold, Ohio, came to assist with mending clothes. Soon members of other Mennonite churches in Fulton and Lucas counties began visiting twice a month to help; this tradition continues to the present day. By 1960, the Sunshine Children's Home had a capacity of around 100 children, but by then, Roy Engler had retired after forty years with the Wabash Railroad and Georgette was having health problems. On June 28, 1960, an agreement turned over ownership of Sunshine Children's Home to the Mennonite Board of Missions, with a thirteen-member board of trustees. The agreement stipulated that a residence would be available to the Engler children as long as they lived and that Sunshine would assist with their care if at all possible.

The Sunshine Children's Home continued to grow under the Mennonites' leadership. Mennonite churches across Ohio and Indiana raised money for major projects, programs, equipment, and special events for residents through a popular bazaar and quilt auction which began in 1974. In 1978 (despite some resistance from neighbors), Sunshine opened its first group home, the Parkridge Lane Family Care Home. This was the first group home in Toledo for adults with developmental disabilities, and the first of many to allow them to live in a community setting as independently as possible. In 1983, the Family Support Program began as a children's daycare center at Sunshine Children's Home and eventually expanded to include family resource services, intervention services, community recreation, a respite house, as well as crisis intervention services.

By 1985, Sunshine began providing consulting services to the Association of Retarded Citizens of Fulton County and took over operation of its family-care home. Two years later, Sunshine took over emergency operation of three family-care homes in Toledo. The board changed the facility's name to Sunshine Inc., in 1994, in recognition that while still serving children, the majority of individuals in the family-care homes and supported living were now adults. From that time, Sunshine Children's Home referred specifically to the original facility on Maumee Western Road.

Roy Engler died in 1973, Georgette in 1975, and their four remaining children by 1997.

Bittersweet Farms

When Bettye Ruth Kay became a teacher in 1973 for the first Toledo Public Schools' class for autistic children, she quickly learned that "we would not 'cure' my students' autism, so I talked with parents and professionals about what might be done to plan for these students' lives after they left school."[15] In 1975, she visited England's Somerset Court, a community for autistic adults. That trip inspired her to help create the Autistic Community of Northwest Ohio two years later, as a non-profit organization for the purpose of providing residential treatment for adults with autism. The following year, the group received a grant from the Ohio Department of Mental Retardation to purchase land and build a residence for fifteen autistic adults.

In the summer of 1981, the Bittersweet Farms Life Skills day program began as a one-year pilot program jointly funded by the Ohio Department of Agricultural Education and the Toledo Public Schools' Department of Adult Education. The name, Bittersweet Farms, was selected because a wild bittersweet vine was found on the eighty-acre farm in Whitehouse, but also in recognition of the bittersweet lives of those with autism. Less than two years later, a fifteen-bed residential home was built; Bittersweet Farms was licensed by the state as an intermediate-care facility. Activities such as animal husbandry, horticulture, woodworking, and gardening are used as therapy for the residents.

After only six years of operation, Bittersweet Farms encompassed seven buildings and had a staff of nearly thirty with an annual budget of $1 million. Bettye Ruth Kay died in 1996, but the farm continues to offer a unique opportunity for autistic adults.

Zeigler Habilitation Homes

In addition to Sunshine and Bittersweet Farms, other residential programs in northwest Ohio serve persons with developmental disabilities. Zeigler Habilitation Homes was founded by Charlotte Zeigler in 1977; a location on Vance Street in Toledo served as the organization's first group home.[16] Charlotte Zeigler died in 2005, but her family continues her work helping persons with developmental disabilities and mental illness through its group homes.

CUSTODIAL INSTITUTIONS TO COMMUNITY CARE

Endnotes

1. For more information on the evolution of care for the developmentally disabled, see James W. Trent, Jr., *Inventing the Feeble Mind: A History of Mental Retardation in the United States* (Berkeley, California: University of California Press, 1994).
2. Trent, 40-59.
3. Pearl S. Buck, *The Child Who Never Grew* (New York: J. Day Co., 1950), 57.
4. Dale Evans Rogers, *Angel Unaware* (Westwood, New Jersey, 1953).
5. *Fourth Annual Report of the Trustees and Superintendents of the Ohio State Asylum for the Education of Idiotic and Imbecile Youth* (Columbus, Ohio: R. Nevins, state printer, 1861), 18.
6. Elliott Howard Gilkey, *The Ohio Hundred Year Book: A Handbook of the Public Men and Public Institutions of Ohio from the Formation of the North-west Territory (1787) to July 1, 1901* (Columbus, Ohio: F. J. Heer, state printer, 1901), 713-714.
7. Gilkey, 714.
8. For more information on the creation of the Lott School and Lott Industries, see the Josina Jones Lott Collection, MSS-186, WMCC.
9. Minutes of the First Convention of the National Association for Parents and Friends of Mentally Retarded Children, 1950. Lucas County Board of Mental Retardation and Developmental Disabilities.
10. Minutes of the Board of Trustees of the Lott Sheltered Workshop Foundation of Lucas County, Inc., 1956-1958. Lucas County Board of Mental Retardation and Developmental Disabilities.
11. For more information on the creation of educational programs for the developmentally disabled children of Wood County, see scrapbooks of the Wood County Board of Mental Retardation and Developmental Disabilities, in the custody of the Wood County MRDD Board.
12. For more information on GOAL for the Profoundly Retarded and the Decem Center, see the Josina Lott Collection, MSS-186, Box 1, folder 8; and Box 5, WMCC.
13. Esther B. Peachey, *50 Years of Sunshine: An Anniversary History, 1950-2000* (Maumee, Ohio: Sunshine, Inc., 2000).
14. Peachey, 11.
15. For more information on the history of Bittersweet Farms, see Bittersweet Farms Records, MSS-195, WMCC.
16. For more information on the history of Zeigler Rehabilitation Services, Inc., see MSS-208, WMCC.

Josina Lott at the sheltered workshop she founded

The original minutes of the first meeting of the board of trustees of the Sheltered Workshop Foundation of Lucas County, Inc., April 18, 1956 (From the Lucas County MRDD Board)

Students in the first class for developmentally disabled children in Wood County, 1956. The classes were held in Ridge School, Bowling Green (From the Wood County MRDD Board)

Advertisement in support of a tax levy to support services for developmentally disabled children, 1968

Carl Schmidt Motor Sales donated the use of a station wagon to the Wood County Association for Retarded Children in 1956. The car provided transportation for students attending Ridge School (From the Wood County MRDD Board)

Bettye Ruth Kay, ca. 1980

The headquarters of the Lucas County Board of Mental Retardation (established in 1967) on Collingwood Avenue in Toledo

50 Years of Sunshine: An Anniversary History 1950-2000, by Esther Peachey

The annual report of the Ohio State Asylum for the Education of Idiotic and Imbecile Youth, 1861

Toledoan Jay Shuer, middle, with Congressman Lud Ashley, left, 1965. Shuer was active in the establishment in 1950 of the National Association of Parents and Friends of Mentally Retarded Children, and also active in the creation of the Lucas County parents' association

Groundbreaking for the Larc Lane School, 1962

Groundbreaking for the Wood Lane School, 1971 (From the Wood County MRDD Board)

A student at Wood Lane School, ca. 1972 (From the Wood County MRDD Board)

Chapter 7

"HIRE THE HANDICAPPED"
Vocational Rehabilitation for Disabled Persons

Barbara L. Floyd

Promoting the employment of the handicapped involves two main activities: placing the disabled person in a suitable job, and educating the employer and the general public to the fact that the handicapped are employable.

Shirley Roeger, University of Toledo
graduate student, 1962

The first federal program to help people with disabilities by providing vocational rehabilitation services was signed into law in 1920 by President Woodrow Wilson. Prior to its passage, only disabled veterans were assisted by the federal government; they were given minimal pensions following the Civil War. Without federal assistance, those with disabilities were forced to look to the states for help. Some states, like Ohio, provided significant services, especially to disabled children. But most did not. World War I, and the huge number of disabled veterans it produced, changed this.

Ohio Congressman Simeon D. Fess and Georgia Senator Hoke Smith pushed for the passage of the new law. It was significant because "for the first time the national government said, without justification on patriotic grounds, that public funds should be used to help disabled people rise above their disabilities."[1] While the new law was a step forward, it was written in such a way that it had to be reauthorized every four years. It did not become permanent until the enactment of the Social Security Act of 1935.

Just before World War II began, the federal government pushed for more employment opportunities for disabled persons, particularly veterans. In 1941, a National Conference on the Employment of the Handicapped presented positive reasons for employers to hire disabled workers.[2] The conference noted studies showing that disabled workers had less absenteeism and suffered fewer accidents on the job than able-bodied workers. Regardless, most employers continued to resist hiring disabled people. The national conference confirmed what many persons with disabilities believed: the reason they were not hired was deeply rooted prejudice against them.

"HIRE THE HANDICAPPED"

One exception was the Ford Motor Company, where founder Henry Ford had a policy of non-restrictive employment; in 1941, the company employed nearly 2,000 physically disabled persons. The World War II labor shortage temporarily improved disabled workers' employment outlook, as men who had been judged unfit to serve were hired by war industries. For many companies, it was the first time that they had hired disabled workers.

In 1943, Congress passed the LaFollette-Barden Act which created advanced rehabilitation services for both veterans and civilians. The act established a cost share for rehabilitation programs between the federal government and the states and included, for the first time, services for physical and mental restoration in addition to vocational rehabilitation. The National Council on Rehabilitation expanded its definition of rehabilitation that year to state, "Rehabilitation is the restoration of the physically handicapped to the fullest physical, mental, social, vocational, and economic usefulness of which they are capable."[3]

In 1947, the President's Committee on the Employment of the Handicapped was established. The committee's goal was to educate the public on the need to employ people with disabilities. One activity of the committee was to sponsor a yearly "Employ the Physically Handicapped Week," celebrated in Toledo for the first time that year. The primary motivation for the "Hire the Handicapped" campaigns of the post-war era was not altruistic. Rather, proponents of vocational rehabilitation sought to move disabled people off social welfare and charity and into paying jobs where they could support themselves. One outgrowth of this push for economic independence, however, was the desire of many disabled persons to also become physically independent, with the same rights as the rest of Americans.

The aftermath of the Korean War led to further expansion of vocational rehabilitation efforts by the federal government and the states. In 1954, President Dwight Eisenhower created the Office of Vocational Rehabilitation within the Department of Health, Education, and Welfare, and increased the amount of money provided by the federal government to the states to seventy-five percent of the cost of rehabilitation. The law set up a multi-program approach to disability and rehabilitation which included grants to states, grants for research, and training grants for those who provided rehabilitation services. Eisenhower justified the expansion of the federal government's role and budget by stating, "We are spending three times as much in public assistance to care for non-productive disabled people as it would cost them to become self-sufficient and taxpaying members of their community. Rehabilitated people as a group pay back in federal income taxes many times the cost of their rehabilitation."[4]

Between 1950 and 1967, the federal rehabilitation budget grew from $20.5 million to $500 million. In 1956, Congress offered assistance to those who were beyond rehabilitation by creating a safety net called Social Security Disability Insurance (SSDI). This program provided a federal cash benefit to workers who could no longer perform work because of a disability. With the creation of Medicare in 1965, those eligible for SSDI also received comprehensive health insurance.

Toledo's Efforts to Hire the Handicapped

Two studies, in 1948 and 1962, that looked at employers and persons with disabilities, reveal much about the successes, and failures, of northwest Ohio to assist disabled persons to find work. The first study, undertaken by University of Toledo graduate student William McLennand following the end of World War II, surveyed employers' attitudes toward hiring persons with disabilities.[5] The 1962 study, done by UT graduate student Shirley Roeger, surveyed disabled people to understand their perspective on vocational rehabilitation.

McLennand's 1948 study estimated there were between 38,000 and 75,000 disabled people in northwest Ohio. Twelve percent of Ohioans seeking employment had some degree of disability. But of these, statistics showed that the Ohio State Employment Service referred only four percent to employers, and only 1.7 percent of these individuals were eventually hired. Most of those placed were veterans. Persons with epilepsy and blindness had the most difficulty finding employment, while those with orthopedic disabilities had the easiest time. But despite such small numbers of successful placements, the businesses that did employ persons with disabilities reported they were overwhelmingly satisfied in terms of the quality of work, dependability of the workers, and compatibility with the work environment. McLennand also found that although most employers had positive attitudes in the abstract about hiring disabled workers, when pushed to actually hire such workers, they were much less favorably disposed to the idea.

Shirley Roeger's 1962 study was unique in that she surveyed disabled persons rather than their employers or prospective employers. Roeger herself was a disabled person with cerebral palsy.[6] Her estimate of disabled northwest Ohioans was similar to McLennand's: about 45,000 disabled persons in Lucas County and about 33,000 of those in Toledo. She based her statistics on national population figures and extrapolated the northwest Ohio figures. These estimates included over 1,000 amputees, over 7,000 deaf people, and nearly 2,000 with epilepsy.[7]

Roeger's study examined governmental and non-governmental employment opportunities for disabled people. She surveyed seventy-five disabled persons and concluded that physical independence, parental care, academic and occupational training, and compassion of employers were key to the quality of life. While some received public or family assistance, most who were employed were able to fully support themselves. Those who worked in their training area were the most satisfied. Roeger's study also revealed some personal stories. One subject with cerebral palsy lived in Toledo with her parents until they divorced. Then she was placed in a mental institution, where she remained for over twenty years. At the age of forty-two, she returned to Toledo and got a job at a sheltered workshop, where she received her first occupational and academic training.

Roeger noted several organizations were employing disabled workers in 1962, although most were charitable organizations such as Goodwill Industries. Goodwill Industries of America Inc. was founded in Boston in 1902 by Edgar J. Helms, a Methodist minister. Driven by compassion for the downtrodden, Helms sought to improve the quality of life for these individuals. He traveled to the wealthier parts of Boston and requested donations of used clothing and other items, then recruited poor men and women to restore them. In the mid-1930s, Goodwill narrowed its focus to "assisting persons with disabilities, not with charity, but with vocational testing, job training, and personal development programs aimed at competitive employment."[8]

In 1933, Charles W. Graham, pastor of Toledo's Central Methodist Church, convened a small meeting of local clergymen who voted to create a "barter and exchange" program as well as a free employment bureau for the poor.[9] Incorporated as Organized Goodwill Inc., the group was one of eight Ohio Goodwill organizations. In 1934, the group changed its name to Goodwill Industries of Toledo, Inc. Like its parent organization, the local chapter sought to "help persons who were unemployed, or underemployed, due to some personal barrier to employment," including physical, mental, emotional, social, behavioral, and learning disabilities, and homelessness. Graham served as the first president.[10]

Goodwill's services for individuals with disabilities were divided into two parts, vocational rehabilitation and industrial contracting. The retail sales division, created in 1933, provided employment opportunities for individuals who refurbished donated items that were then sold to the public. In 1950, Goodwill Industries of Toledo launched its industrial contract services division to provide jobs and training opportunities by subcontracting with businesses and industries. By 1956, as vocational rehabilitation became more accepted, Goodwill expanded by creating a work evaluation department, adding a janitorial training program in 1957 and a clerical school in 1963. In the 1980s, the organization opened a commercial print shop and a food service training program. Recently, Goodwill Industries of Northwest Ohio (its current name) has operated an online auction site on the World Wide Web.

Other Toledo charitable organizations that work to employ persons with disabilities included the Salvation Army, Society of St. Vincent de Paul, Volunteers of America, and the Conlon Center. The latter organization was named for the bus driver who transported students to Feilbach School. The Conlon Center taught typing and duplication skills to people with severe disabilities.

Because she was a UT student, not surprisingly Roeger discussed the university's disability services. "Handicapped students attend the University of Toledo, and provisions are made for their comfort and convenience. Special parking permits, elevator keys, and ramps at building entrances are provided. Students help with transportation, note taking, and other personal needs. Faculty members are thoughtful in making special arrangements for tests, papers, and recitations," Roeger noted.[11] Roeger's observations are in keeping with comments of UT President William Carlson, who gave several speeches on disability issues during his presidency (1958 to 1972). In a 1959 speech before the Rotary Club of Toledo, Carlson stated, "[disabled students] never ask for any favors. All they ask for is a chance. They do not look for an easy way as do some who are more fortunate. They ask only that they have the opportunity of shaping themselves in accordance with standards of excellence."[12]

Roeger concluded her study by calling for additional studies of Toledo's disabled community. "These and similar studies could do much to awaken the general public to the needs and liabilities of the disabled, so that the individual with a physical impairment could more easily find a useful, productive place in society," Roeger stated.[13]

The White House Conference on Handicapped Individuals, 1977

In 1974, the U.S. Congress passed the "White House Conference on Handicapped Individuals Act" as part of the Rehabilitation Act amendments of that year. Congress noted that nearly one-sixth of the nation's population was disabled, and "it is of critical importance to this nation that equality of opportunity, equal access to all aspects of society, and equal rights guaranteed by the Constitution of the United States be provided to all individuals."[14] To achieve this goal, Congress directed the president to establish the first-ever White House Conference on Handicapped Individuals, held in May 1977. The conference assessed the problems of disabled people, created general awareness about the issues, and made recommendations to the president and Congress on how to improve the lives of disabled persons.

Nearly 4,000 people attended the conference; 142 proposals were made by the delegates in the areas of health, education, social, and economic concerns. For the first time, the discussion of disability issues at the national level went beyond vocational rehabilitation. Slogans like "Hire the Handicapped" were no longer enough. Most importantly, the conference recognized that disabled people and their caregivers had to be involved at the highest levels of decision and policy making on disability issues.

Coinciding with the Independent Living Movement, and immediately following protests by disabled activists against President Jimmy Carter's Health, Education, and Welfare Secretary Joseph Califano, the conference signaled that major changes were underway in how people with disabilities would be treated. Yet disabled people continued to struggle to have equal employment opportunities. The federal publication, "Out of the Job Market, A National Crisis," published by the President's Commission on the Employment of the Handicapped in 1986, noted that while the economy was healthy and unemployment declining, the percentage of disabled persons who were unemployed in 1986 was larger than it had been in 1970.[15]

Endnotes

1. U.S. Department of Health, Education, and Welfare Social and Rehabilitation Service Administration, *50 Years of Vocational Rehabilitation in the U.S.A., 1920-1970* (Washington D.C.: Government Printing Office, 1970), 3-4.
2. William J. McLennand, "An Investigation into Employers' Attitudes Toward Employment of the Handicapped in the City of Toledo, Ohio," master's thesis, the University of Toledo, 1948, 13.
3. McLennand, 4
4. President Dwight D. Eisenhower, as quoted by John Lenihan in *Performance: Bicentennial Issue*, the President's Committee on the Employment of the Handicapped, XXVII (November-December 1976-January 1977), 68.
5. See McLennand's thesis for details on his survey and its results.
6. Shirley A. Roeger, "A Study of the Relationship Between the Training and Employment of Handicapped Adults in the Toledo Metropolitan Area," master's thesis, the University of Toledo, 1962.
7. Roeger, 7.
8. Scrapbook, Goodwill Industries of Northwest Ohio, ca. 1950s-1970s. Privately held, in the collection of Goodwill Industries of Northwest Ohio.
9. Roeger, 39.
10. Scrapbook, Goodwill Industries of Northwest Ohio, ca. 1950s-1970s.
11. Roeger, 35.
12. William S. Carlson, "Toledo Employs the Physically Handicapped," speech before the Rotary Club of Toledo, October 1, 1959. William S. Carlson Papers, UM 14, University of Toledo Archives, Box 6, Folder 4, WMCC.
13. Roeger, 96.
14. *Summary Final Report, The White House Conference on Handicapped Individuals* (Washington D.C.: the Government Printing Office, 1977), 3. Lee Lawrence Papers, MSS-174, Box 6, Folder 9, WMCC.
15. "Out of the Job Market: A National Crisis," The President's Commission on the Employment of the Handicapped, 1986. Lee Lawrence Papers, MSS-174, Box 6, Folder 9.

"HIRE THE HANDICAPPED"

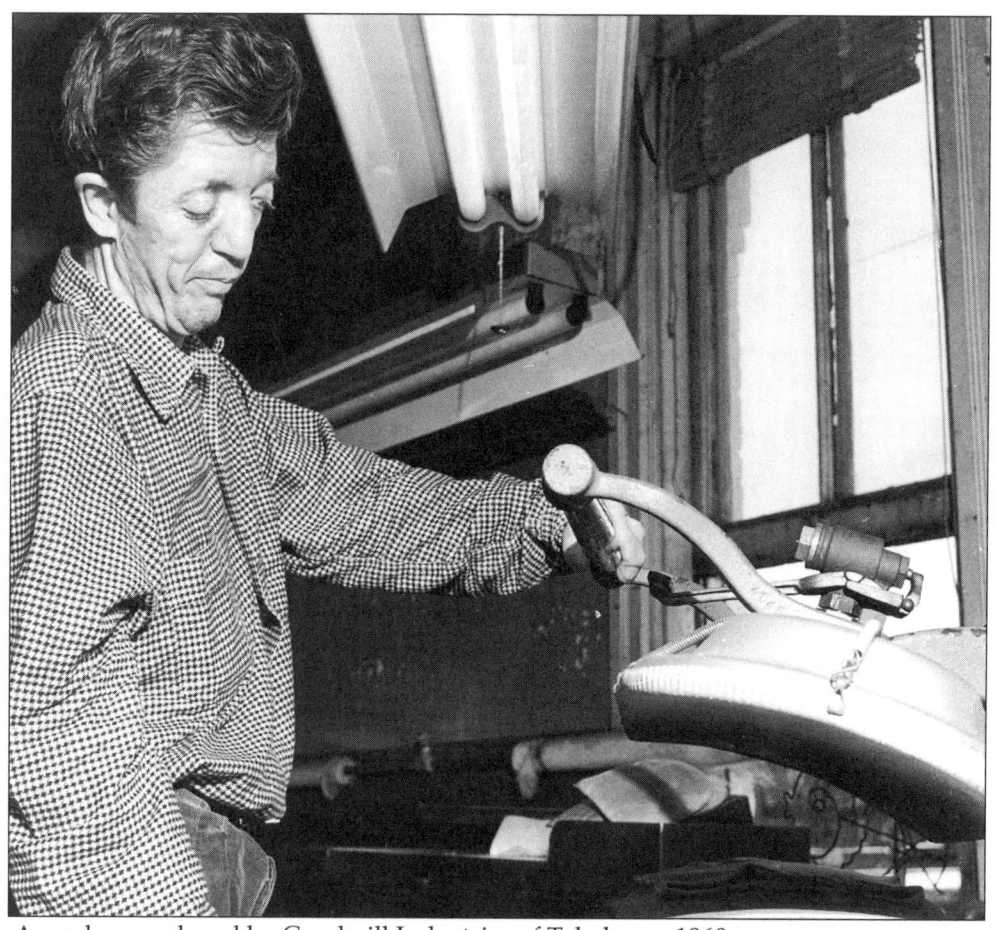

A worker employed by Goodwill Industries of Toledo, ca. 1960
(From Goodwill Industries of Northwest Ohio, Inc.)

An advertisement from Tommy Sexton, a disabled worker, ca. 1962. Sexton contracted polio at the age of 16, and spent time at Warm Springs, Georgia, before returning to Toledo

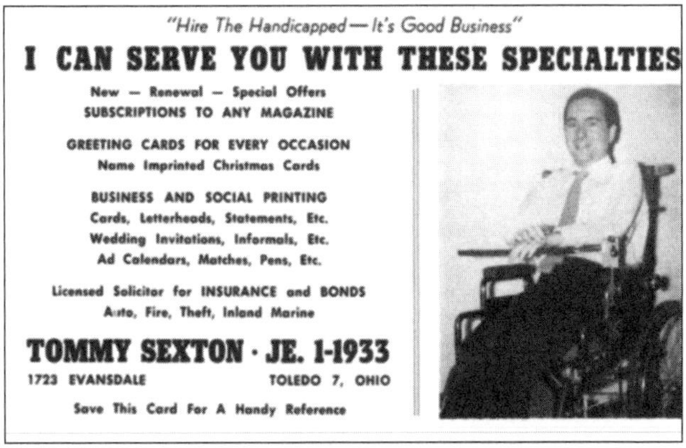

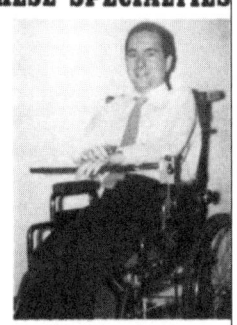

"Hire The Handicapped — It's Good Business"

I CAN SERVE YOU WITH THESE SPECIALTIES

New — Renewal — Special Offers
SUBSCRIPTIONS TO ANY MAGAZINE

GREETING CARDS FOR EVERY OCCASION
Name Imprinted Christmas Cards

BUSINESS AND SOCIAL PRINTING
Cards, Letterheads, Statements, Etc.
Wedding Invitations, Informals, Etc.
Ad Calendars, Matches, Pens, Etc.

Licensed Solicitor for INSURANCE and BONDS
Auto, Fire, Theft, Inland Marine

TOMMY SEXTON · JE. 1-1933
1723 EVANSDALE   TOLEDO 7, OHIO
Save This Card For A Handy Reference

Donations to Goodwill Industries, ca. 1950

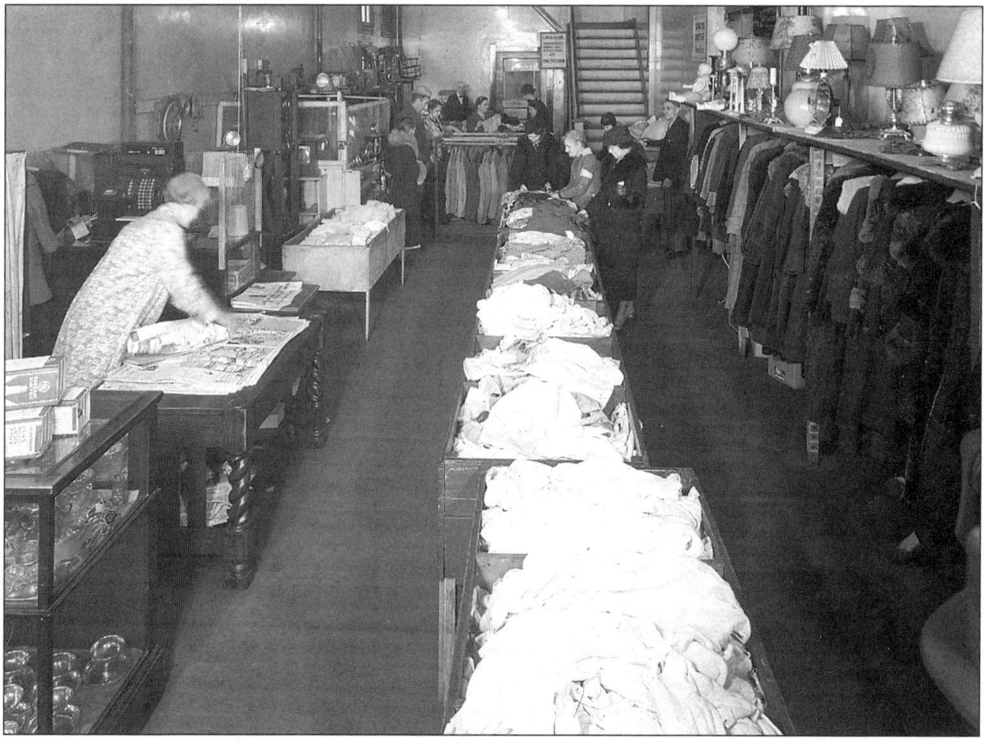

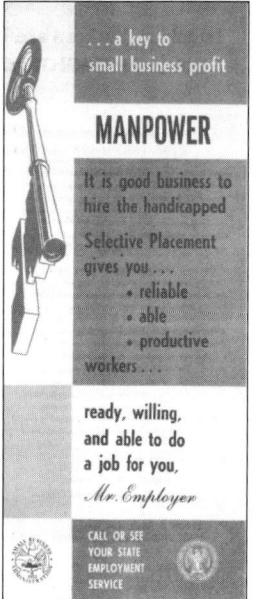

One of the Goodwill retail stores located in Toledo, ca. 1940 (From Goodwill Industries of Northwest Ohio, Inc.)

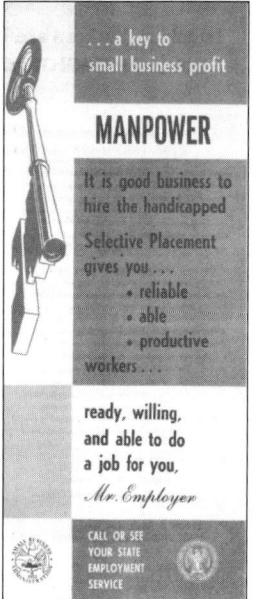

Promotional brochure from the Small Business Administration to encourage the employment of disabled workers, ca. 1962

An advertising brochure for the Conlon Service Center, ca. 1962

Goodwill Industries, located on North Huron in Toledo. The building was named the Morral Building in honor of William W. Morral, who donated $10,000 to Goodwill in 1938 (From Goodwill Industries of Northwest Ohio, Inc.)

Goodwill Industries retail store in Toledo, ca. 1950 (From Goodwill Industries of Northwest Ohio, Inc.)

The program from the first White House Conference on Handicapped Individuals, 1977

THE WHITE HOUSE

WASHINGTON

April 29, 1977

To the Participants in the White
   House Conference on the Handicapped

Your presence here attests to your deep concern for the well-being of millions of mentally or physically handicapped fellow citizens.

I assure you that your efforts will have my Administration's full cooperation and support.

You have a great deal of hard work ahead of you. But the realization that you are working for such a worthwhile cause should lighten your task, and the knowledge that so many Americans share your commitment should give you encouragement and strength.

I look forward to your recommendations and hope that your sessions will be highly productive and rewarding for those you serve.

Jimmy Carter

President Jimmy Carter's letter to participants of the White House Conference, 1977

Chapter 8

OVERCOMING OBSTACLES
From Deinstitutionalization to Independent Living

Barbara L. Floyd and Tamara Jones

The stimulation of campus life, the challenge of study, the companionship of a wide range of new friends, has a wonderful effect on many young men and women when they come to college. But none finds this more stimulating than the handicapped student. He sees here a way to make the most out of the powers that God has given him—and often these are splendid talents, perhaps a kind of compensation for the physical cross he must bear.

University of Toledo President William S. Carlson, 1959

This could get very expensive if every university is going to provide a higher level of support for handicapped students. There has to be a better way to accomplish this task!

UT President Glen Driscoll to Ohio Board of Regents' chancellor William Coulter, 1984

After centuries of virtual home imprisonment or large-scale institutional care, people with disabilities finally began to see major changes. There are several reasons for this post-World-War-II paradigm shift. First, vocational rehabilitation programs aimed at training disabled persons, particularly veterans, to be financially self-supporting gave some the resources to live independently for the first time. "Hire the Handicapped" may have been a public relations slogan, but it integrated disabled persons into the job market, thus helping them gain wider social acceptance.

Second, the parents' movement of the mid-1950s meant that caregivers no longer felt alone as they assumed active and vocal roles in determining the best care for their children. Parents and caregivers advocated for public school education over state institutional care, which opened doors for the integration of all disabled children into local schools.

Third, improvements in medical care, particularly the use of antibiotics, meant that many disabled people now lived much longer. Hence, political leaders—particularly those opposed to large, expensive government programs—had a financial incentive to move disabled people to independence so they would not rely on government support. In addition, medical advances in the mental health field led to the development of new psychotropic drugs that helped many who might have been institutionalized to live at home.

Fourth, deinstitutionalization as a policy of state and federal governments emptied the large custodial institutions, returning disabled persons to their communities. Unfortunately, many found that needed services were not always available. Lastly, and most importantly, people with disabilities themselves began to speak out and advocate for their own independence. They demanded full integration into society, particularly complete access to public services, the removal of architectural barriers, and an end to employment discrimination.

Removing Obstacles

In 1963, polio survivor Hugh Gregory Gallagher worked as an assistant in the Washington office of Alaska Senator Bob Bartlett. In his position, Gallagher frequently conducted research at the Library of Congress. Access to the library was through a heavy, revolving door, reached after climbing five high steps.[1] Obviously the library was not accessible to persons in wheelchairs like Gallagher. He noticed, however, that the back doors had only one shallow step and that it would be easy to add a ramp, making the building accessible. Gallagher wrote a letter to Quincy Mumford, the librarian of Congress, requesting such a ramp. Mumford hesitated, claiming that the architect of the Capitol would have to be consulted first. Senator Bartlett called the librarian and demanded that the ramp be built. As a result, the Legislative Appropriations Act of 1964 included a provision for $5,000 to build the ramp at the rear of the library.

Gallagher's first small victory led to others. Next, he turned his attention to the National Gallery of Art, not quite as difficult to navigate as the Library of Congress. He still felt that a small ramp would allow better access. Gallagher wrote to Museum Director John Walker, asking for a ramp. Walker refused, saying a ramp was not necessary because a guard was always on duty to assist anyone who needed help getting inside. Wanting to be able to enter and exit buildings under his own power, Gallagher decided to use himself as a test case to prove how difficult it was for disabled visitors to get inside. On a cold, snowy Saturday, he wheeled himself to the bottom of the steps and sat with a watch to see how long it would take the guard to notice him. The guard stayed at the security desk during inclement weather, so anyone needing help was not visible.

Gallagher's plan was foiled when two tourists noticed him and carried his chair up the stairs, but he was not finished. He wrote more letters to Walker, who then claimed that the architectural integrity of the building would be ruined by a ramp and that Gallagher would have to consult the board of trustees (and its chairman, Supreme Court Chief Justice Earl Warren) if he wanted something done about it. Gallagher did just that, writing a letter to the board, which ultimately approved the ramp. A temporary one was built, but it would be another twenty-five years before a permanent structure was put in place.

Gallagher continued his fight, ensuring that national parks and hospitals were also made accessible. He and Bartlett forced the Kennedy Center for the Performing Arts to be built as an accessible building. The defining moment of his activism came when he tried to secure accessibility to the Smithsonian Institution. Writing in Bartlett's name, Gallagher sent several letters to the secretary of the Smithsonian, S. Dillon Ripley. Ripley was so uncooperative that Gallagher decided—with Bartlett's support—to draft legislation requiring that all buildings built entirely or partially with federal funds be accessible to everyone. He also wanted the bill to be framed in the context of civil rights.

Despite efforts by Mary Switzer, head of the federal Office of Vocational Rehabilitation, to intervene, Bartlett sent the bill to the Appropriations Committee for approval. The [Lyndon] Johnson administration opposed it, however, fearing that it would cost too much. Gallagher, Bartlett, and supportive senators persisted, and the bill was eventually approved by both houses of Congress. That summer, the Architectural Barriers Act of 1968 became law. It would eventually pave the way in 1990 for the Americans with Disabilities Act (ADA).

In Pursuit of Reasonable Accommodations: Section 504

Following passage of the Architectural Barriers Act, disability rights activists continued their efforts to gain legal protections. In 1973, Congress passed the Rehabilitation Act, but only after President Richard Nixon twice vetoed it. Of the bill's four sections, Section 504 was the most far-reaching because it promised civil rights for disabled persons.[2] The impetus for Section 504 began in 1972 when Congress failed to add a disability provision to the Civil Rights Act of 1964. Some lawmakers still thought it might be possible to attach that provision to another bill. Members of the Senate Welfare Committee did so, adding language from Title VI of the Civil Rights Act to the final draft of the Rehabilitation Act of 1973. The new provision became Section 504.

The fight for Section 504 had begun in the late 1960s with James Cherry, a severely disabled student who attended Howard University Law School. As a white student in a mostly African-American school, Cherry noticed parallels between the struggle for racial civil rights and the fight for equal rights by disabled persons. The school's administration did not agree and denied Cherry's request for a parking space near the building where his classes were held, as well as a key to the elevator.

After passage of Section 504 in 1973, Cherry began writing to the Department of Health, Education, and Welfare (HEW) to have Section 504 regulations issued so that he might make his case. He filed a lawsuit against HEW Secretary David Mathews to force the regulations; in 1976, the court ruled in Cherry's favor. By the time the ruling was handed down, Jimmy Carter had been elected and Joseph Califano was the new secretary of HEW.

Because President Carter had promised to listen to and aid disabled people, the community expected more of him than the Nixon administration. The American Coalition of Citizens with Disabilities met with Califano shortly after Carter took office because it felt the new administration was not moving fast enough to get the Section 504 regulations signed. The Coalition threatened action if this was not done quickly.

On April 5, 1977, demonstrations began after last-minute negotiations between disability leaders and Califano broke down. Califano wanted additional time to study the regulations, but activists worried he was looking for ways to weaken the legislation. The disability community staged demonstrations and sit-ins at each of the HEW regional offices. In San Francisco, the sit-in lasted twenty-five days. Califano finally signed the Section 504 regulations on April 28 as well as the regulations for the Education for All Handicapped Children Act. The fight over Section 504 had united disability activists into a national movement.

Disability Activism Leads to the ADA

Many of the efforts to gain equal rights for disabled people were organized by activists on college campuses who used 1960s civil rights and Vietnam War protestors' methods. Among these activists was college student Ed Roberts, who started the movement for independent living. Paralyzed by polio at fourteen, Roberts completed most of high school at home by means of a phone connected to his classroom. After high school, he wanted to attend the University of California at Berkeley, but had to sue to gain admission, which he did in 1962. But the school's dorms were not able to accommodate his iron lung, so Roberts was given housing in the Cowell Hospital. In time, other quadriplegics began attending Berkeley and living in the hospital. Roberts and his companions created a unique atmosphere in their ward.

Inspired by the 1964-5 Free Speech Movement on the Berkeley campus, Roberts and other disabled students began agitating for equal rights. He founded the Disabled Students Program as well as the Rolling Quads, a political activism group that fought for wheelchair access, accessible housing, and wheelchair repair. The Rolling Quads eventually moved out of Cowell Hospital into the community to be independent. Under Roberts's leadership, the group formed the Center for Independent Living (CIL) in 1972, an agency governed by and for people with disabilities. One unique regulation stipulated that at least fifty-one percent of the staff and the board of directors had to have a disability. Because of Roberts' efforts, disabled persons living independently became common in Berkeley. Eventually, all fifty-eight California counties had satellite centers for independent living and hundreds more CIL offices were founded throughout the country.

With the success of the CIL movement, Roberts continued his crusade. In 1983, he founded the World Institute on Disability with the help of Judith Heumann, who would later become U.S. assistant secretary of education in the [Bill] Clinton administration. The non-profit organization was dedicated to helping disabled people achieve independence and an improved quality of life.

One of the more vocal—and controversial—disability rights organizations was ADAPT. Founded in the mid-1970s, ADAPT grew out of efforts to help severely disabled persons in nursing homes to live independently. The organization encouraged disabled people to use direct confrontation to achieve their goals. Most of ADAPT's early efforts focused on equal access to public transportation, but after passage of the 1990 Americans with Disabilities Act, the group dealt mainly with independent living.

Surprisingly, the ADA was the work of two Republican administrations generally opposed to expanding government regulation. In 1982, President Ronald Reagan dismissed all of President Carter's appointees to the National Council on Disability, the organization that advised the president on disability issues. But Reagan soon discovered that disability rights issues transcended political ideology. Even under Republican leadership, the council issued a report that year recommending adding disability to the provisions of the Civil Rights Act of 1964. Some in the disability community were opposed to this, believing that disability discrimination was distinctive, and therefore required a separate civil rights bill.

Four years later, the council issued a new report, "Toward Independence: An Assessment of Federal Laws and Programs Affecting Persons with Disabilities—With Legislative Recommendations," that outlined legal changes to make transportation accessible and to end discrimination in employment for disabled workers. This report served as the basis for an early version of the ADA, which was defeated in 1988. The 1990 version, overwhelmingly approved by both houses of Congress, was different in that the law now required people with disabilities to file complaints and lawsuits as a means to monitor compliance with its requirements.

The ADA made it illegal to discriminate against disabled people in employment, and required reasonable accommodations to make buildings accessible. Unlike Section 504, the ADA extended its regulations to the private sector. On July 26, 1990, the ADA was signed into law by President George H.W. Bush. In 2008, an expansion of the ADA was approved by Congress and signed by President George W. Bush.

The Disability Rights Movement in Northwest Ohio

The mission of the Toledo Society for Crippled Children had changed several times from its 1920 founding: from overseeing a crippled children's school, to building a convalescent home, to running a children's hospital, to operating a kindergarten for disabled children.[3] After the kindergarten closed in 1974, the Society once again needed a new mission. At its annual meeting that year, the articles of incorporation were amended to state that the group would support the construction of a building for "the charitable care of crippled or otherwise physically handicapped children and adults." Thus, for the first time, the organization began to address the needs of disabled adults as well as children. To reflect its new mission, the organization changed its name to the Toledo Society for the Handicapped. Land was purchased on Monroe Street in Sylvania Township; a local architectural firm was hired to design an accessible building.

In 1978, Dr. Maurice Newberger, a trustee, described his experience visiting the Center for Independent Living, founded by Ed Roberts in Berkeley, California. He noted that the Center was "completely controlled and operated by handicapped individuals," and suggested that the Society consider creating such a center.[4] As a first step, he suggested establishing a program advisory committee consisting exclusively of disabled people. The board agreed that its current representation of twenty to twenty-five percent disabled persons was insufficient.

On May 18, 1980, the new building was dedicated. The organization began to move away from a focus on providing charitable services to become more activist in its programs. It joined with Barrier Free Toledo to celebrate Handicapped Awareness Week. It advocated for improved public transportation, arguing that under Section 504, this was the responsibility of the Toledo Area Regional Transit Authority, not the Society, which had been providing much of Toledo's disability transportation. In recognition of its new activist agenda, in 1981, the Society amended its articles of incorporation to add advocacy in its mission.

But to many, the mission of the organization still remained unclear. It was not until 1986 that the Society's long-range planning committee presented a resolution suggesting that the Society officially become a Center for Independent Living. The committee also suggested a change in the group's name to reflect this new mission. By 1988, the word "handicapped" had negative connotations. Recruiting new employees had become difficult because the Society's name implied it was not committed to disability rights. Current employees with disabilities found it demeaning to be associated with the organization with a name that included "for the handicapped" because it represented the sort of custodial, protective care that had defined disability services for centuries. The parents of potential students hesitated to send their children to its programs in fear that they would be identified with an organization whose name focused on limitations rather than abilities. To correct these perceptions, the board recommended changing the name to the Ability Center of Greater Toledo, which was officially adopted in 1989.[5] The organization began to change its programming to reflect the goals of an independent-living center and reconstitute its board of trustees to include a majority of disabled persons.

Reflecting what was happening nationally, the Ability Center staff participated in and supported local, state, and national disability rights protests. One of its most heated battles involved the University of Toledo and a 1989 plan to construct an on-campus housing complex for fraternities and sororities. Joining with Barrier Free Toledo and the Northwest Ohio Chapter of the National Spinal Cord Injury Association, the Ability Center sued the university because architectural plans for the buildings called for disabled access to only the first floor of the residences. Neither the recreation area in the basement nor the upper levels of living space would be accessible without assistance.

The university contended that installing elevators in the buildings would add significantly to the cost and that the buildings met state accesibility standards. The Ohio Rehabilitation Services Commission joined in opposition to the construction plans.

Just before the suit was to be heard in U.S. District Court, the university and groups reached a settlement that provided access not only to fraternity and sorority housing, but also set aside funding to improve accessibility to other dormitories on campus.

But a year after the settlement was reached, the Ability Center continued to see problems with implementing the agreement. "It is our view that the vast majority of the provisions of the settlement agreement pertaining to the on-campus sorority and fraternity housing have been either totally ignored, or approached in a totally unsatisfactory manner," Richard Gunden, president and CEO of the Ability Center, stated in a 1990 letter to UT President Frank Horton.[6]

The Ability Center continued in its leadership role in fighting for equal access for disabled persons. In 1992, Ed Roberts visited the Center and held a seminar on the new Americans with Disabilities Act. In keeping with the organization's more activist role, the job of the executive director now included political lobbying on behalf of disabled people; the staff took positions in many national organizations that advocated for accessibility and equal rights. The Center's board supported health-care reform in the early 1990s and opposed physician-assisted suicide in 1996. Today, the Ability Center remains active in advocating for disability rights and continues to provide independent living skills training, information and referrals, and peer support services to disabled people living in the seven northwest Ohio counties.

Disability Rights at the University of Toledo

As the fraternity and sorority housing controversy indicated, the University of Toledo struggled to provide equal access to its buildings and services. In many ways, UT's experience was a microcosm of the issues confronted by many institutions and organizations in meeting the independence needs of people with disabilities.

In the 1950s and 1960s, the university addressed disabled students on an ad hoc basis. Individuals received special keys to elevators that were off limits to the general population. Arrangements were made for assistance in notetaking and access to buildings where no elevators existed. Because of the relatively small number of UT disabled students, these arrangements were not unusual for the time. In 1967, the university architect conducted an assessment to identify architectural barriers in the university's buildings and prepared a plan to remedy the problems. But little happened as a result of the report.

In the 1970s, the disabled students on campus found an advocate in Art

Edgerton, UT's director of affirmative action. In 1975, Edgerton, who was disabled himself, proposed that the dean of students create an advisory board to identify issues of disabled students and develop uniform policies for addressing accessibility. It took two years to create the advisory board, the Handicapped Affairs Coalition. Carolyn Eagle, a graduate student, was assigned to the committee, and her position evolved to full-time coordinator of the Office of Handicapped Student Services. The advisory board became the Advisory Committee for Handicapped Students and included faculty and students.

In 1981, when the university threatened to abolish the Office of Handicapped Student Services, the committee and others wrote letters in support of its programs. The committee's effort was joined by a vocal and active Handicapped Students' Association. The following year, the committee passed a unanimous resolution calling on UT to adapt all current buildings to make them accessible and require all new buildings to be completely accessible. The committee and the Office of Handicapped Student Services worked closely together to try to bring UT into compliance with Section 504.

But problems persisted. In 1982, when a committee to develop special admission requirements for disabled students was established, Art Edgerton protested. He argued there should be no "special" admission requirements for disabled persons, but rather uniform admission standards for all students. The following year, a student fell out of her wheelchair while attempting to go up a steep ramp on the fifth floor of University Hall. A hearing-impaired student complained about being told to sit in the back with his interpreter, not close enough to read the instructor's lips. Faculty were frustrated as well with the lack of standardized policies and services. In 1983, Dr. Bernard Bopp, a professor of physics and astronomy, wrote to the vice president of student affairs about the university's "meanness" toward disabled students because UT lacked even basic programs for assistance.[7]

In August 1983, Carolyn Eagle prepared "Proposal: Comprehensive Services for Handicapped Students at the University of Toledo,"[8] a report for President Glen Driscoll. It called for the creation of a resource center and additional positions of coordinator for hearing-impaired students and a coordinator of adaptive education. Driscoll was not swayed by the proposal. "I have read the proposal for the creation of a Handicapped Student Services Center submitted by Carolyn Eagle. It will not surprise you to learn my reaction is pretty negative," Driscoll said in a memorandum to the vice president for student affairs.

"I sympathize with the handicapped students, and I think society ought to service them if it is going to admit them to public universities . . . [but] until the State provides support, or until you choose to rearrange your own budget, I will resist adding additional funds to provide services for the handicapped student except as University Legal Counsel advises me are required by law," Driscoll concluded.[9] He forwarded his comments to the chancellor of the Ohio Board of Regents, suggesting that it would be more cost-effective to make "a very few campuses as the center where such support will be provided rather than trying to equip every single campus." When the Ability Center of Toledo filed its lawsuit over the fraternity and sorority housing in 1989, *The Blade* noted that the Governor's Office for Advocacy for People with Disabilities reported receiving more complaints about UT accessibility issues than any other public university in the state.

Services for students gradually expanded and improved. In 1987, the Advisory Committee for Handicapped Student Services completed a report on learning disabilities, concluding that the university must also develop support services for students affected by such disabilities. In 1989, Office of Handicapped Student Services changed its name to the Center for the Physically and Mentally Challenged. In 1992, the name changed again to the Office of Accessibility. With new services, the number of UT disabled students increased from sixty-seven in 1987 to over 1,000 in 1994. The office now offers comprehensive services, including note taking, reading, and interpreting. The current enrollment of disabled students at UT is estimated at around 2,000.

Help from Man's Best Friend

As people with disabilities increasingly sought to be independent, new approaches developed to provide the assistance that made such independence possible. Guide Dogs for the Handicapped Inc., a training program for assistance dogs, was founded in 1984 by Joe and Pamela Maxwell in Columbus, Ohio, so that Joe, a quadriplegic, would be less dependent on his wife.[10] The organization became a non-profit two years later and soon expanded throughout the country.

In 1989, the name was changed to Assistance Dogs of America, Inc. (ADAI) because the board of directors felt use of the word "handicapped" was offensive and "guide dogs" was inaccurate, as this implied that only the visually impaired were served by the organization. That same year, ADAI moved its national training headquarters to Swanton in northwest Ohio. The organization currently serves those within a 250-mile radius of the Toledo area.

ADAI's purpose is to "bring together a dog in need of a home and a disabled person in need of assistance." Clients include those with cerebral palsy, spina bifida, multiple sclerosis, muscular dystrophy, rheumatoid arthritis, and stroke. Dogs placed with clients help with daily tasks such as alerting to doorbells and phones, helping to maintain balance, and traveling up and down stairs. The trained dogs enable clients to live their lives on their own terms. By interacting with the community at school assemblies and civic gatherings, ADAI educates the public about disability, disability stereotypes, and barriers to independence.

Endnotes

1. Hugh Gregory Gallagher recounts his fights to gain access to federal buildings in his book *Black Bird Fly Away: Disabled in an Able-Bodied World,* (Arlington, Virginia: Vandamere Press, 1998), 105-127.
2. The history of the disability rights movement is detailed in Doris Zames Fleischer and Frieda Zames's book *The Disability Rights Movement: From Charity to Confrontation* (Philadelphia: Temple University Press, 2001).
3. For more information on the history of the Toledo Society for the Handicapped and its successor, the Ability Center of Toledo, see the Ability Center of Toledo Records, MSS-190, WMCC.
4. Minutes of the Toledo Society for the Handicapped, May 18, 1978. Ability Center of Toledo Records, MSS-190, Box 7, Folder 15.
5. The change in the name of the organization occurred after the January 5, 1989 meeting of the board of directors. See minutes in the Ability Center of Toledo Records, MSS-190, Box 8, Folder 2.
6. University of Toledo Archives, vertical files on fraternity and sorority housing, WMCC.
7. Memoranda from B.W. Bopp to Lancelot C.A. Thompson. University of Toledo Archives, Vice President for Student Affairs Administrative Files, UR 88/63, Box 8, Folder 10, WMCC.
8. University of Toledo Archives, Office of the President Subject Files, PA/92, Box 50, Folder 27, WMCC.
9. Letter from Glen R. Driscoll to Lancelot C.A. Thompson, October 20, 1983. University of Toledo Archives, Office of the President Subject Files, Box 50, Folder 27.
10. For more information on the history of the Guide Dogs for the Handicapped, Inc., and its successor, the Assistance Dogs of America, Inc., see the Assistance Dogs of America, Inc. Records, MSS-175, WMCC.

A disability rights protest in Toledo, ca. 1990

A disability rights protest over architectural barriers in downtown Toledo, ca. 1990

Toledo Society for the Handicapped transportation buses, ca. 1981. The society provided much of the transportation for the city's disabled at the time

Groundbreaking for the new Toledo Society for the Handicapped building on Monroe Street, 1979

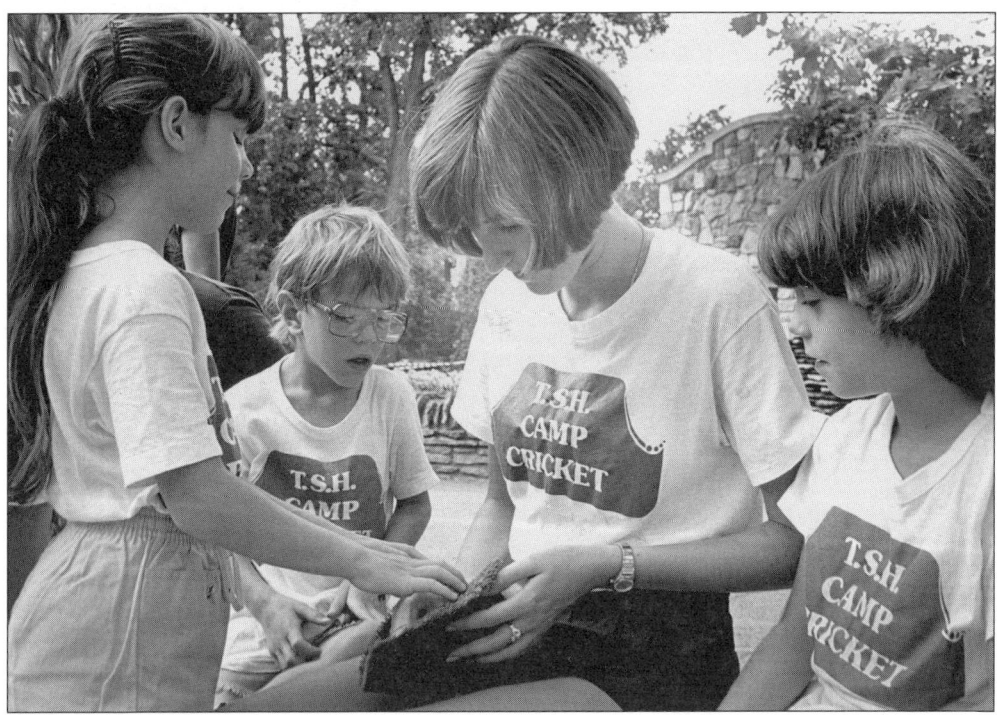

Participants in Camp Cricket, a Toledo summer camp for both disabled and able-bodied children, ca. 1985

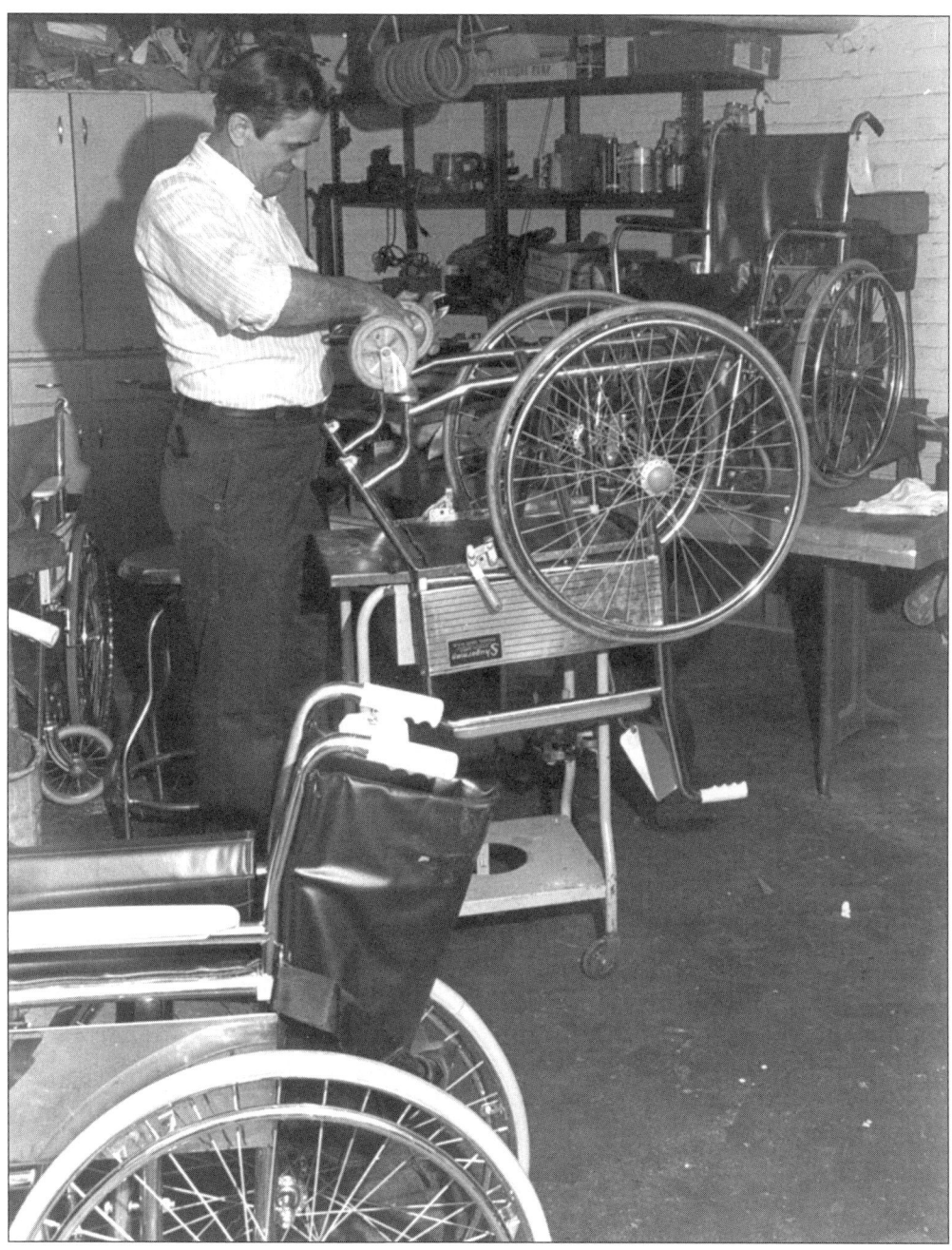
Repairing wheelchairs at the Toledo Society for the Handicapped, ca. 1985

A participant in a disability rights protest in downtown Toledo over enforcement of the ADA, ca. 1990

Training an assistance dog, ca. 1990

Promotional brochure advertising the services of the Ability Center, ca. 2000

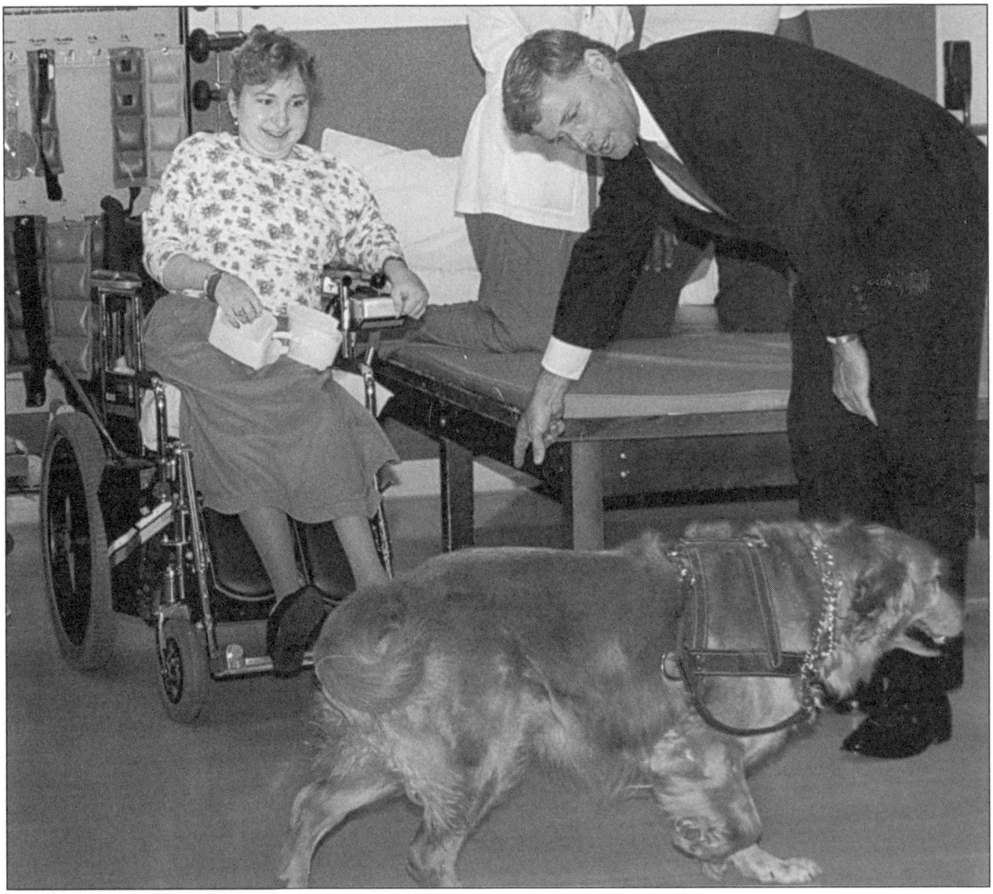

Shelley Papenfuse introduces her assistance dog to Vice President Dan Quayle, ca. 1990

Many ADAI dogs are claimed from local humane societies

Chapter 9

WHO FITS THE LABEL OF "DISABLED?"
THE HISTORICAL MEANING OF DISABILITY

By Barbara L. Floyd

In brief, not only for its own sake, but for the benefit of Society as a whole, every crippled child has the right to the best body which modern science can help it secure; the best mind which modern education can provide; the best training which modern vocational guidance can give; the best position in life which his physical condition, perfected as it may be, will permit; and the best opportunity for spiritual development which its environment affords.

The "Crippled Child's Bill of Rights,"
passed at the tenth annual convention
of the International Society for Crippled Children,
Cleveland, 1931

The way American society has treated people with disabilities has changed as our values, awareness, understanding, and knowledge have evolved. Today when we read Dorothea Dix's 1840s reports of mentally ill persons chained to walls in jail cells, we are appalled. When we see the comments of the superintendent of the Ohio School for the Deaf in 1917 asking how people with disabilities can be allowed to reproduce, we are offended. When persons with developmental disabilities are labeled by the state as "imbecile" or "feeble-minded"—or, more recently, "retarded"—we recoil.

The disability rights movement has done much to sensitize us about the labeling and treatment of people with disabilities. In turn, disability history has begun to sensitize us to the largely unknown historical experience of disabled persons. It would be difficult to imagine our nation's history told today without a discussion of the important role of women, African-Americans, Native Americans, or immigrants. As our history is richer with the inclusion of these groups, so too will it be expanded and deepened by including the historical experience of disabled people. As disability historian Douglas Baynton stated, "Disability is everywhere in history, once you begin looking for it, but conspicuously absent in the histories we write."[1] Historians engaged in this new field's research must continue to search out information and educate the public about the mostly anonymous lives of those who, for centuries, lived behind closed doors. We must learn about all of the Alva Bunkers in our history. We must also learn more about the work of organizations that sought to help persons with disabilities.

But an examination of disability history also makes clear that the very meaning of disability is constantly in flux, which confounds our understanding of that history. Some disabilities are now treated effectively with medication; the afflicted may no longer fit society's current definition of a disabled person. For example, many who would have once spent their lives in state hospitals labeled as insane live freely today with appropriate medications. Epilepsy, which in the early twentieth century meant confinement in a state institution, is now treatable. Polio no longer exists in our country. Eye surgery can correct maladies such as cataracts that once meant certain blindness. If we cannot decide who is to be labeled as disabled, how can we hope to understand the history of disability?

HIV/AIDS—A Disability?

In recent years, one disability that has been dramatically redefined is that of human immunodeficiency virus/acquired immune deficiency syndrome. HIV/AIDS was once not just a disability, but a certain death sentence. In Toledo, NOVA (No One's Victory Alone) started in 1984 as a grass-roots effort to train volunteers to help people infected with HIV/AIDS by providing needed social services and support.[2] Toledoan David Gercek, diagnosed with AIDS, realized that in addition to assistance with everyday matters, many of those with the disease also needed housing. In 1989, a former rectory was purchased to provide such housing, named David's House Compassion in Gercek's memory following his death. It served as a residence for those in northwest Ohio in the last stages of HIV/AIDS. In 1992, NOVA merged with David's House, and became the only area HIV/AIDS service organization. Funds to operate the program came from the U.S. Department of Housing and Urban Development, the Ohio Department of Health, various local agencies, and from the Ryan White C.A.R.E. Act, which provided federal funds for HIV/AIDS programs. Over the fifteen years of its existence, David's House assisted hundreds of HIV/AIDS patients and their families.

Like many people with disabilities throughout history, those with HIV/AIDS experienced discrimination and stigmatization. When it was unclear how the disease was spread, the infected were feared in the way those with polio had been feared in the 1940s and 1950s. And once the means of transmission were verified, discrimination became worse as those with the disease were blamed for what many saw as unwise lifestyle choices. Typical of the response was that of a group called the AIDS-ALL Prevention Center, which described itself as "an educational non-profit tax exempt public charity." The group distributed informational stickers to college campuses around the country that were intended to be attached to restroom doors. The stickers read "AIDS KILLS—one mistake and you could be dead."[3] A 1994 study of the disease in Lucas County found that most cases were contracted through homosexual sex and intravenous drug use; such studies fueled discrimination.[4] Those with the disease fought back, and HIV/AIDS became as much a civil rights issue as a medical issue.

But as medical science developed potent drugs to combat the effects of HIV/AIDS, those once labeled disabled were able to live with the disease with no visible disability. As a result of the changes in HIV/AIDS treatment, David's House Compassion closed its doors in 2004. While some of its services continue to be offered by other social service agencies, its residential component is not. Just as the Opportunity Home that provided residential care for Toledo polio patients was no longer needed after the polio vaccine was developed, David's House was no longer needed with changes in the treatment of HIV/AIDS.

Diseases such as polio and HIV/AIDS, along with many mental and neurological illnesses, are no longer seen as disabilities because of advances in medical science. We have, however, a rapidly aging population whose mobility limitations will add hundreds of thousands to our definition of disabled. And while whole new groups of people are being defined as having a disability, some whom society still judges to be disabled do not define themselves as such. The National Federation of the Blind believes blindness is an inconvenience, not a disability. And as medical science makes some disabilities more tolerable, other people with disabilities rebel against the medical model that defines disability as something in need of a cure. Many in the deaf community believe surgical implants that can restore aspects of hearing are an affront to their unique deaf culture. Actor Christopher Reeve, who spent his last years looking for a cure for spinal cord injuries, was often criticized by the disability community for his single-minded push for medical research to correct his disability rather than accepting it.

So how has disability historically been defined and how does that definition impact how society treats people with disabilities? Clearly, our definition of disability as well as our responses to disability are ever changing. Perhaps the best way for society to address the issue is to ensure that whoever is defined as disabled has rights equal to those defined as able-bodied. As disability scholars Doris Zames Fleischer and Frieda Zames stated, "People with disabilities is the

WHO FITS THE LABEL OF "DISABLED?"

only protected class that anyone can enter at any time through birth, accident, illness or advanced age."[5] Protecting and promoting the rights of the disabled ultimately means protecting and promoting the rights of everyone. And incorporating the historical experience of people with disabilities into our history as a nation will lead to greater understanding among us all.

Endnotes
1. Douglas C. Baynton, "Disability and the Justification of Inequality in American History," in *The New Disability History: American Perspectives*, Paul K. Longmore and Lauri Umansky, eds., 52.
2. For more information on the history of Toledo's response to HIV/AIDS, see David's House Compassion Records, MSS-188, WMCC.
3. University of Toledo Archives, Office of the President Subject Files, PA/92, Box 128, Folder 1, WMCC.
4. Lucas County HIV Prevention Community Plan, 1994-1996, in David's House Compassion Records, MSS-188, Box 4, Folder 63.
5. Doris Zames Fleischer and Frieda Zames, *The Disability Rights Movement: From Charity to Confrontation*, (Philadelphia: Temple University Press, 2001) 215.

AIDS KILLS — one mistake and you could be dead!

Learn how to protect yourself from "Public Health Enemy #1"
PRESIDENT RONALD REAGAN

Use the Free "FAST-FACT-FONE"™ → Dial 1-800-FACT-911
IN FLORIDA ONLY 305-533-LIFE

Take a minute - Save a life - yours!

AIDS-ALL™ PREVENTION CENTER A Division of LIFE/HEALTH Centers of America®
AN EDUCATIONAL NON-PROFIT TAX EXEMPT PUBLIC CHARITY
© 1987

A restroom door sticker distributed to college campuses across the country, 1987, typical of the anti-AIDS hysteria of the time

NOVA, No One's Victory Alone, was a voluntary organization providing basic social services to those with HIV/AIDS

David's House Compassion was a residence providing housing for those with end-stage AIDS

About the Authors

Barbara L. Floyd is the director of the Ward M. Canaday Center for Special Collections at the University of Toledo. She is also the University of Toledo archivist. She holds a bachelor's degree in journalism, a master's in American history, and a MPA in public administration, all from the University of Toledo.

Kimberly Brownlee is the manuscripts librarian and assistant university archivist at the Ward M. Canaday Center for Special Collections. She received a bachelor's degree in American history from the University of Toledo. She also holds a master's of library and information science and a graduate certificate in archival administration, both from Wayne State University.

Tamara Jones is administration assistant in the Ward M. Canaday Center for Special Collections. She received her bachelor's degree from Kenyon College in international studies and a master's of information science from the University of Michigan.

Jennifer Free is a fourth-year doctoral student in American history at the University of Toledo. She received her bachelor's degree in history from the University of Northern Colorado. She also holds a juris doctor degree from the University of Toledo College of Law and is a member of the Ohio Bar.

David G. Chelminski is an online instructor of history, geography, and political science at Lourdes College in Sylvania, Ohio, and worked for six years in the Ward M. Canaday Center for Special Collections. He holds a Ph.D. in history from the University of Toledo and a master's in information science from the University of Michigan.

From Institutions to Independence—
A Timeline of Disability Laws and Regulations

1864 The Enabling Act is signed by President Abraham Lincoln and authorizes the Columbia Institution for the Deaf and Dumb and Blind to confer college degrees.

1869 The first wheelchair patent is registered with the United States Patent Office.

1883 In his book, *Essays in Eugenics*, Sir Francis Galton coins the term "eugenics" to describe his science of "improving the stock" of humanity."

1890s- 1920s Progressive reformers advocate for the creation of state workers compensation programs.

1911 Congress passes a joint resolution to investigate the issues of workers' compensation and employer liability for monetary awards to disabled workers.

1918 Congress enacts the Smith-Sears Veterans Rehabilitation Act to promote the return to civilian employment of veterans discharged from the military due to a disability.

1920 Congress enacts the Fess-Smith Civilian Vocational Rehabilitation Act to create a vocational rehabilitation program for disabled persons.

1924 The Commonwealth of Virginia enacts a law permitting the forced sterilization of individuals determined to be "feebleminded, insane, depressed, mentally handicapped, epileptic and other."

1927 In *Buck v. Bell*, the United States Supreme Court rules that the forced sterilization of people with disabilities does not violate their fundamental rights as prescribed by the Constitution. Following the Court's decision, 27 states initiate the wholesale sterilization of "undesirables."

1933 Franklin D. Roosevelt becomes the first disabled president. During his presidency, he embarks on a campaign of "splendid deception" to minimize the extent of his disability.

1935 In New York City, the League for the Physically Handicapped protest discrimination by the Works Progress Administration. League members stage a nine-day sit in.

Congress passes the Social Security Act, which includes assistance to blind individuals and disabled children and extends vocational rehabilitation programs.

1936 Congress enacts the Randolph-Sheppard Act for the employment of blind vendors in the lobbies of federal office buildings.

1938 Congress enacts the Fair Labor Standards Act increasing the number of sheltered workshop programs for blind workers.

1943 Congress enacts the LaFollette-Barden Act which expands vocational rehabilitation programs and provides funds for health care services.

1945 President Harry S. Truman establishes an annual National Employ the Handicapped Week.

1947 The first meeting of the President's Committee on National "Employ the Handicapped Week" is held in Washington. Publicity campaigns stress the competence of people with disabilities.

1950 The Social Security Amendments of 1950 establish a federal-state program to aid permanently and totally disabled individuals.

1952 The President's Committee on Employment of the Physically Handicapped becomes a permanent organization reporting to both the President and Congress.

1956 The Social Security Amendments of 1956 create the Social Security Disability Insurance (SSDI) program for disabled workers aged 50 to 64.

1958 The Social Security Amendments of 1958 extend SSDI benefits to dependents of disabled workers.

1961 President John F. Kennedy appoints a President's Panel on Mental Retardation to investigate the status of persons with mental retardation and is instructed to develop rehabilitation programs.

The American National Standard Institute publishes standards for making buildings accessible to the physically handicapped.

1963 In an address to Congress, President Kennedy calls for a reduction in the number of institutionalized persons and a return to community care for the mentally ill and developmentally disabled. The Mental Retardation Facilities and Community Health Centers Construction Act authorizes grants for the construction of community mental health centers.

1964 President Lyndon B. Johnson signs the Civil Rights Act of 1964.

1965 Congress creates the Medicare and Medicaid programs. It also passes the Vocational Rehabilitation Amendments of 1965 authorizing federal funding for rehabilitation facilities and the creation of the National Commission on Architectural Barriers to Rehabilitation of the Handicapped.

1966 President Johnson establishes the President's Committee on Mental Retardation.

1968 Congress enacts the Architectural Barriers Act mandating that federally owned facilities be accessible to people with physical disabilities.

1970 Congress passes the Urban Mass Transit Act and mandates that all new mass transit vehicles be equipped with wheelchair lifts.

1972 The Social Security Amendments of 1972 create the Supplemental Security Income (SSI) program, relieving families from the financial responsibility of caring for adult disabled family members.

The Commonwealth of Virginia ends its sterilization program.

1973 Enactment of the Rehabilitation Act of 1973 marks the single greatest achievement of the disability rights movement to date. Section 504 prohibits programs receiving federal funding from discriminating against the disabled. Disability rights activists see the law as a powerful device and make the signing of regulations to implement Section 504 a priority.

1975 Congress enacts the Education for All Handicapped Children Act mandating that state supported schools provide disabled students with a "free appropriate public education in the least restrictive environment."

1976 An amendment to the Higher Education Act of 1972 authorizes services to students with physical disabilities who are entering college.

1977 Joseph Califano, secretary of HEW, refuses to sign regulations for Section 504 of the Rehabilitation Act of 1973. Demonstrations take place in ten cities, including San Francisco, where 150 demonstrators refuse to disband. Califano finally signs the regulations.

1978 Title VII of the Rehabilitation Act Amendments of 1978 authorizes the first federal funding for independent living centers.

1980 Congress passes the Social Security Amendments of 1980, which result in hundreds of thousands of individuals with disabilities losing their benefits.

The Civil Rights of Institutionalized Persons Act authorizes the United States Justice Department to file civil law suits on behalf of residents of institutions whose rights are allegedly being violated.

1981 The Telecommunications for the Disabled Act mandates telephone access for deaf and hearing impaired people in public places.

1984 In response to complaints from people whose Social Security benefits have been terminated, Congress passes the Social Security Disability Reform Act.

The Voting Accessibility for the Elderly and Handicapped Act mandates that polling places be accessible.

1986 *Toward Independence*, a report published by the National Council on the Handicapped, outlines the legal status of Americans with disabilities and documents discrimination.

1988 The Fair Housing Act Amendments Act adds people with disabilities to those groups protected by federal fair housing legislation.

Congress passes the Technology-Related Assistance Act for Individuals with Disabilities, authorizing federal funding to state programs designed to facilitate access to assistive technology.

1989 The President's Committee on Employment of the Handicapped is renamed the President's Committee on Employment of People with Disabilities.

1990 On July 26, President George W. Bush signs the Americans with Disabilities Act during a ceremony attended by thousands of disability rights advocates. The act provides comprehensive civil rights protection for individuals with disabilities.

Congress also passes the Ryan White Comprehensive AIDS Resource Emergency Act to assist communities in dealing with the growing HIV/AIDS epidemic.

1996 Senator Robert Dole becomes the first person with a visible disability since Franklin Roosevelt to run for president of the United States. Georgia voters elect Max Cleland, who was physically disabled in Vietnam, to the United States Senate.

2001 The Commonwealth of Virginia House of Delegates approves a resolution expressing remorse for its eugenics practices dating from 1924 to 1979.

Terminology

18th Century
Cripple
Insane
Idiot
Imbecile
Lunatic
Mad
Deaf and dumb
Blind
Fool
Simpleton
Cretin
Deranged
Neurotic
Phobic

19th Century
Cripple
Deaf and dumb
Insane
Fool
Idiot
Lunatic
Mongoloid
Abnormal
Defective
Cretin
Epileptic
Pauper (insane)
Psychopathic
Feeble-minded
Imbecile
Simpleton

Early 20th Century
Backward
Defective
Insane
Dullard
Fool
Idiot
Silent
Imbecile
Lunatic
Mentally retarded
Mongoloid
Moron
Neurotic
Pauper
Subnormal
Cripple
Feeble-minded
Mentally ill
Spastic

Late 20th Century
Handicapped
Emotionally and
    behaviorally disturbed
Learning disabled
PTSD (Post Traumatic
    Stress Disorder)
Mentally ill
Down Syndrome
Mentally handicapped
Mentally retarded
Polio
Autistic

Schizo
Manic Depressive
Bi-polar Psychotic

21st Century
"Person who is …"
Partially sighted
Differently abled
Mentally ill
Chronically ill
Congenitally disabled
Developmentally
    disabled
Learning disabled
Mobility disabled
Non-vocal, non-verbal
Visually impaired or
    blind
Deaf or hard of hearing
Epileptic
Of short stature
Emotionally disabled
A wheelchair user
"Person who has …"
Special needs
A speech disability
A communication
    disability

Primary Sources from the collections of the Ward M. Canaday Center at the University of Toledo

Ability Center of Toledo Records, MSS-190.

Bittersweet Farms Records, MSS-195.

David's House Compassion Records, MSS-188.

Family Service of Northwest Ohio Records, MSS-075.

Hugh Gregory Gallagher Papers, MSS-185.

Josina Lott Papers, MSS-186.

Quota International of Toledo Records, MSS-129.

Rotary Club of Toledo Records, MSS-145.

Sight Center of Toledo Records, MSS-179.

University of Toledo Archives, Office of the President Subject Files, PA/92.

University of Toledo Archives, Vice President for Student Affairs Administrative Files, UR 88/63.

SELECTED BIBLIOGRAPHY
Secondary Sources

Bromberg, Walter. *From Shaman to Psychotherapist: A History of the Treatment of Mental Illness.* Chicago: H. Regnery, 1975.

Burch, Susan. *Signs of Resistance: American Deaf Cultural History, 1900 to World War II.* New York: New York University Press, 2002.

Cox, Clyde. *History of Toledo State Hospital.* Self-published, 1964.

Gallagher, Hugh Gregory. *By Trust Betrayed: Patients, Physicians, and the License to Kill in the Third Reich.* Arlington, Virginia: Vandamere Press, 1995.

Gallagher, Hugh Gregory. *FDR's Splendid Deception: The Moving Story of Roosevelt's Massive Disability and the Intense Efforts to Conceal it from the Public.* FDR Memorial Edition, Arlington: Vandamere Press, 1999.

Koestler, Frances A. *The Unseen Minority: A Social History of Blindness in the United States.* New York: David McKay Company, Inc., 1976.

Longmore, Paul K. *Why I Burned My Book and Other Essays on Disability.* Philadelphia: Temple University Press, 2003.

Longmore, Paul K. and Lauri Umansky, eds. *The New Disability History: American Perspectives.* New York: New York University Press, 2001.

Oshinsky David M. *Polio: An American Story.* Oxford: Oxford University Press, 2005.

Trent, James W. *Inventing the Feeble Mind: A History of Mental Retardation in the United States.* Berkeley, California: University of California Press, 1994.

Van Cleve, John Vickrey, ed. *Deaf History Unveiled: Interpretations of the New Scholarship.* Washington, D.C.: Gallaudet University Press, 2002.

Yanni, Carla. *The Architecture of Madness: Insane Asylums in the United States.* Minneapolis, Minnesota: University of Minnesota Press, 2007.

Zames Fleischer, Doris and Frieda Zames. *The Disability Rights Movement: From Charity to Confrontation.* Philadelphia: Temple University Press, 2001.

INDEX

Ability Center of Greater Toledo, vii, ix, x, 137-138, 140, 146
Abrams, Robert E., 68
Academy of Medicine of Toledo and Lucas County, 80
Accessibility standards, 158
ADAPT, 135
ADA--See Americans with Disabilities Act
Administration building, Toledo State Hospital, 19
Advisory Committee for Handicapped Students, University of Toledo, 139
AIDS-ALL Prevention Center, 153-154
Alcoholism, 9
Allen, Edgar, 49-51, 54
Amblyopia, 29
American Ayslum, Hartford, CT, 30
American Federation for the Blind, 26
American Printing House for the Blind, 24
Americans with Disabilities Act, 133, 135-136, 138, 161
Amputees, 117
And They Shall Walk: The Story of Sister Elizabeth Kenny, 76
Angel Unaware, 96
Anne Grady Center, 101
Anne Grady Services, 101
Annie's House, 101
Antibiotics, 131
Architectural barriers, 132-133, 138, 159-160
Architectural Barriers Act of 1968, 133, 159
Archives, v
Archivists, vi
Aristotle, 61
Assistance Dogs of America Inc., 140-141, 146-147
Assistive technology, 160
Association of Retarded Citizens of Fulton County, 102

Asylum for the Education of the Deaf and Dumb, 30
Autism, 103
Autistic Community of Northwest Ohio, 103
Awl, William, 24

Barrier Free Toledo, 137
Bartlett, Senator Bob, 132-133
Baseball team, Toledo State Hospital, 18
Baynton, Douglas, iv, 151
Beaudry, George, 38
Bell, Alexander Graham, 24, 31, 35
Birmingham School and polio vaccine, 80
Birth control and eugenics, 62-63
Birth defects, 43, 68
Bittersweet Farms, 103
Bittersweet Farms Life Skills day program, 103
Black Bird Fly Away: Disabled in an Able-Bodied World, 77
Black Stork, 63
Blade, Toledo, 30
Blindness, 23-30, 153
Blind—sterilization of, 64
Blood letting, 3
Board of Superintendents, Toledo State Hospital, 9
Bognar, John, 100
Bollinger, Baby, 63
Bopp, Bernard, 139
Boston's disabled, 118
Boy Scouts, Feilbach School, 56
Braille, 23
Brinkerhoff, General Roehliff, 7-8, 17
Broadbecke, John, 44
Bronte, Charlotte, 61
Buck, Pearl S., 96

Bunker, Alva, 46-48, 51-52, 54, 151
Bunker, Charles, 51
Bush, President George H.W., 136, 161
Bush, President George W., 136
Business and Professional Women's Club, 27
By Trust Betrayed: Patients, Physicians, and the License to Kill in the Third Reich, 70

Califano, Joseph, 120, 134, 160
California sterilization law, 64
Camp Courageous, 97
Camp Cricket, 144
Campobello Island, 77
Camps for developmentally disabled, 97
Canaday Center, see Ward M. Canaday Center for Special Collections
Cantor, Eddie, 78
Carl Schmidt Motor Sales, 107
Carlson, William S., 119, 131
Carnegie, Andrew, 31
Carter, President Jimmy, 120, 127, 135
Catawba Island, 28
Cemetery, Toledo State Hospital, 11-12, 19
Center for Independent Living, 135, 136, 137, 146, 160
Center for Physically and Mentally Challenged, University of Toledo, 140
Central Mennonite Church, Archbold, Ohio, 102
Central Methodist Church, Toledo, 118
Chamber of Commerce—See Toledo Chamber of Commerce
Chapel, Toledo State Hospital, 19
Cherry, James, 133, 134
Child Who Never Grew, 96
Children with physical disabilities, 45-52
Children's Hospital of Toledo, 82
Citizens Committee for Retarded Children, 106

Civil Rights Act of 1964, 133, 135, 159
Civil rights for disabled, 116, 132-141, 161
Civil Rights of Institutionalized Persons Act, 160
Civil War, 43
Civil War and disability, 43-44, 53
Cleland, Senator Max, 161
Clerical school, Goodwill Industries of Toledo, 119
Clinton, Hillary, 91
Clinton, President Bill, 82
Columbia Institution for the Deaf and Dumb and Blind, 157
Columbus State Institute for the Mentally Retarded, 98
Community Chest—see Toledo Community Chest
Conlon Center, 119, 124
Cottage system for state mental institutions, 8, 10
Coulter, William, 131
Cowell Hospital, 134-135
Crippled, x
Crippled Children's Movement, 48, 54
Crippled Child's Bill of Rights, 51, 151
Custodial care for developmentally disabled, 98

Darrow, Clarence, 63
Darwin, Charles, 61-63
David's House Compassion, 152-153, 155
Deaf Club—See Toledo Deaf Club,
Deaf Hearing Boy: A Memoir, 32
Deafness, 23-24, 30-32, 117, 153, 160
Deaf-sterilization of, 64
Decem Center, 101
Deinstitutionalization, 132, 160
Dementia, 9
Depression, 27, 28

Detached ward system—see Cottage system
Developmental disabilities, 94-111
Dickens, Charles, 61
Diocese of Toledo, 82
Disability as label, 149-154
Disability history, 152, 154
Disability rights protest in Toledo, 142-143, 146
Disability studies, vii
Disability terminology, 163
Discrimination against the disabled, 152, 159-160
District Nurse Association, 43, 46, 48
Dix, Dorothea, 3-4, 17, 95, 151
Dogs used to assist disabled, 140-141, 147
Dole, Senator Robert, 161
Down syndrome, 101
Driscoll, Glen, 131, 139-140
Duty, J.E., 10

Eagle, Carolyn, 139
Easter Seals, 51
Economic independence for disabled, 116
Edgerton, Art, 139
Edison, Thomas, 31
Education for All Handicapped Children Act, 31, 51, 134, 159
Education of the deaf, 30-32
Eisenhower, President Dwight, 116
Electric shock therapy, 10-11
Elyria Rotary, 49
Employ the Physically Handicapped Week, 116
Employment discrimination of the disabled, 132
Employment of disabled, 118
Enabling Act of 1864, 157
Engler, Georgette, 101-103

Engler, Roy, 101-103
Epilepsy, 9, 117, 152
Epileptic—sterilization of, 64
Erskine, William Kellicott, 65, 66
Essay on Population, 62
Essays in Eugenics, 157
Eugenics, 59-69
Eugenics for the developmentally disabled, 96
Eugenics publications, 71
Euthanasia of disabled, 66-68
Euthanasia of disabled children, 67-68
Evans, Dale, 96
Evans, Edward, 26
Ewald, Gottfried, 67
Experimental School for Teaching and Training Idiotic Children, 96
Exposés of treatment of developmentally disabled, 97
Eye screening, 39

Fair Housing Act Amendments Act of 1988, 160
Fair Labor Standards Act, 158
Fallis, Edward O., 8
Family Support Program, Sunshine Children's Home, 102
FDR's Splendid Deception, 78
Federal assistance to disabled, 115-117, 119-120
Feeble-minded, 151
Feilbach School for Crippled Children, 24, 32, 34, 43, 50, 55-57, 81, 82, 119
Feilbach, Charles, 46, 48, 58
Ferris, Jim, x
Fess, Simeon, 115
Fess-Smith Civilian Vocational Rehabilitation Act of 1920, 157
Financial trouble, 9

Fleischer, Doris Zames, 153
Fleischer, Frieda, 153
Ford Motor Company's employment of disabled, 116
Ford, Henry, 116
Fordyce, O.O., 10-11
Fraternity and sorority housing at the University of Toledo, 137-138
Free Speech Movement, 135

Gall, Franz Joseph, 62
Gallagher, Hugh Gregory, 68, 75-79, 82, 91, 132-133
Galton, Sir Francis, 61, 157
Gendron Company wheel chairs, 86
Gercek, David, 152
GOAL for the Profoundly Retarded, 100
Goodwill Industries, 118
Goodwill Industries of Toledo, 118, 122-126
Grady, Anne, 100
Graham, Charles W., 128
Greatest Problem of the Race—Its Own Conservation, 64, 70
Guide Dogs for the Handicapped Inc., 140

Hadamar Psychiatric Institute, Germany, 67
Haiselden, Harry, 63
Handicapped Affairs Coalition, 139
Handicapped Awareness Week, 137
Handicapped Students' Association, 139
Happy Times Club, 26
Harper, Harry, 46
Haverford College, 76
Head injury, 9
Health care reform, 138
Helms, Edgar J., 118
HEW—See U.S. Department of Health, Education and Welfare

Higher Education Act of 1972, 159
Hire the Handicapped campaign, 116-117, 120, 131
Historians, iv, vi
Historical terms for disability, 163
Hitler, Adolph, 66
HIV/AIDS—See human immunodeficiency virus/acquired immune deficiency syndrome
Hoge, Reverend James, 30
Horn, Raymond, 98
Horton, Frank, 138
Hospital School Journal, 47
Howard University Law School, 133
Howe, Julia Ward, 95
Howe, Samuel Gridley, 95
Hubbell, Reverend Horatio N., 30, 31, 35
Human immunodeficiency virus/acquired immune deficiency syndrome, 152-155, 161

Imbecile, x, 151
Independent Living Movement, 120, 129-147
Indiana sterilization law, 64
Industrial contracting for disabled, 118
Infantile paralysis—see Polio
Insanity—see Mental illness
Institution for the Education of the Deaf and Dumb, 30
Institutionalization of developmentally disabled, 96
International Society for Crippled Children, 50-51, 151
Internationale Gessellschaft fur Rassen-Hygiene, Munich, Germany, 66
Iron lung, 75-76

Janitorial training program, Goodwill Industries of Toledo, 119

Jay Shuer School, 99
Jealousy, 9
Johnson, President Lyndon, 133, 159
Jones, John Williams, 64-65
Journal of the American Medical Association, 76
Junior League, 28

Kaufbeuren pyschiatric hospital, Germany, 68
Kay, Bettye Ruth, 103, 108
Keller, Helen, 23-24, 26, 34-35, 47
Kelsey, Ed., 46-48
Kennedy Center for the Performing Arts, 133
Kennedy family and developmental disability, 97
Kennedy, President John F., 158-159
Kennedy, Rosemary, 97
Kenny method for treating polio, 76
Kenny, Sister Elizabeth, 76, 86
Killed-virus vaccine for polio, 80
Kinderhaus, Eglfing-Haar, Germany, 68
Kirkbride design, 8
Korean War, 116

Lactation, 9
LaFollette-Barden Act, 116, 158
Larc Lane School, 100, 111
Lavater, Johann Kaspar, 61
Law for the Prevention of Offspring and Hereditary Diseases, 66
League for the Physically Handicapped, 158
Legislative Appropriations Act of 1964, 132
Libbey, Edward Drummond, 27, 81, 82
Library of Congress, 132
Lincoln, President Abraham, 157
Linton, Simi, v
Lions Club, 25

Lip reading, 31
Live-virus vaccine for polio, 80
Loss of pension, 9
Lott Day School, 99
Lott Sheltered Workshop Foundation, 99
Lott, Josina, 98-100, 105
Love, George R., 10, 65
Lucas County Association for Retarded Children, 99
Lucas County Asylum, 6
Lucas County Board of Mental Retardation, 100, 108
Lucas County Child Welfare Board, 99
Lucas County commissioners, 5, 7
Lucas County General Hospital, 7
Lucas County Hospital, 7
Lucas County Infirmary, 5-7, 20
Lucas County Poor Farm, 4-5

Malthus, Thomas, 62, 63
March of Dimes, 78, 79
Marriage, 9
Massachusetts legislature, 4, 95
Mathews, David, 134
Maumee Valley Hospital, 7
Maumee Valley News, 102
Maumee, Ohio, 5
Maxwell, Joe, 140
Maxwell, Pamela, 140
McLennand, William, 117
McMurtie, Douglas, 45
Medicaid, 159
Medical and Surgical History of the War of the Rebellion, 53
Medical College of Ohio, 7
Medicare, 159
Mennonite Board of Charities, 102
Mental hygiene clinics, 10

Mental illness, 3-12, 131
Mental Retardation Facilities and Community Health Centers Construction Act, 159
Mentally ill—sterilization of, 64
Metrazol, 10
Michigan Child Welfare League, 47
Michigan Hospital School, 46-47
Michigan sterilization law, 64
Milan Conference, 31
Miller, R.H., 32
Mongoloid, 101
Moral treatment, 3, 4
Morral Building, 125
Morral, William W., 125
Mumford, Qunicy, 132
Murphy, Patricia, vii

National Accreditation Council for Agencies Serving the Blind and Visually Impaired, 29
National Association for Parents and Friends of Mentally Retarded Children, 99
National Commission on Architectural Barriers to Rehabilitation of the Handicapped, 159
National Conference on the Employment of the Handicapped, 115
National Council on Disability, 135, 136
National Council on Rehabilitation, 116
National Council on the Handicapped, 160
National Easter Seals Society, 51
National Federation of the Blind, 153
National Foundation for Infantile Paralysis, 78, 80
National Foundation for Infantile Paralysis- See also March of Dimes
National Gallery of Art, 132

National Organization on Disability, 82
National Society for Crippled Children, 50
Nazis, iv
Nazis and eugenics, 66-68
Nearing, Scott, 61, 65, 70
Negative eugenics, 61
New Deal program, 28
New Eyes for the Needy, 29
Newberger, Maurice, 136
Nixon, President Richard, 133
No One's Victory Alone—See NOVA
Northwest Ohio Chapter of the National Spinal Cord Injury Association, 137
Northwest Ohio Psychiatric Hospital, 11
Northwestern Hospital for the Insane, 6, 18
NOVA, 152, 155
Nuremberg trials, 68

Oberlin College, 65-66
O'Connor, Basil, 78
Office of Accessibility, University of Toledo, 140
Office of Handicapped Student Affairs, University of Toledo, 139-140
Office of Vocational Rehabilitation, 116, 133
Ohio Board of Administration, 64
Ohio Board of Regents, 140
Ohio Board of State Charities, 5-7
Ohio Bureau of Services for the Blind, 29
Ohio Chronicle, 31
Ohio Commission for the Blind, 28
Ohio Department of Agriculture, 103
Ohio Department of Education, 25, 31
Ohio Department of Health, 152
Ohio Department of Public Welfare, 25, 31
Ohio General Assembly, 24, 25
Ohio Hospital for Epileptics, 65
Ohio House Bill 200, 1921, 49

Ohio Institution for Feeble-Minded Youth, 64
Ohio Institution for the Education of the Blind, 25
Ohio Plan, 49
Ohio Rehabilitation Services Commission, 137
Ohio Rotary, 49-50, 55
Ohio School for the Deaf, 151
Ohio Senate Bill 174, 1921, 49
Ohio Society for Crippled Children, 49
Ohio State Asylum for the Education of Idiotic and Imbecile Youth, 95, 97-98, 109
Ohio State School for the Blind, 25
Ohio State School for the Deaf, 30-31, 35, 64
Ohio sterilization law, 64
Ohlinger, Gustavus, 51
Old age, 9
Old Ladies' Home, 81
On the Origin of Species, 61-62
One Talent Club, 46
Operation Lazy Eye, 29
Opportunity Home, 80-82, 85, 87-90, 153
Opportunity Kindergarten, 82, 136
Oralism, 23, 31
Organized Goodwill, Inc., 118
Oshinsky, David, 79
Out of the Job Market: A National Crisis, 120
Outdoor relief, 5
Outstanding Deaf Woman of the Year, 32
Overcrowding, Toledo State Hospital, 11

Papenfuse, Shelley, 147
Parents' movement for developmentally disabled, 99, 131
Parents of the Visually Handicapped, 28
Parkridge Lane Family Care Home, 102
Parsons, A. Estelle, 27
Patterson, R.J., 95

Pennsylvania sterilization law, 64
Pensions for disability, 44, 45
Phrenology, 61-62
Physical disabilities, 43-58
Physical disabled—sterilization of, 64
Physiognomy, 61, 62
Poe, Edgar Allen, 61
Polio, 50, 74-91, 134
Polio vaccine in Toledo, 80
Polio: An American Story, 79
Polio—1952 epidemic, 75
Polio—causes of, 75
Poliomyelitis—See Polio
Political excitement, 9
Population control, 62
Positive eugenics, 61
Prejudice against employment of disabled, 115, 117
Prescribed Pediatric Center, 101
President's Committee on the Employment of People with Disabilities, 160
President's Committee on the Employment of the Handicapped, 116, 120, 158, 160
President's Panel on Mental Retardation, 158
Profoundly developmentally disabled, 101
Progressive Club, 26
Progressive era, 44
Progressive movement, 44-45
Project EPIC, 80
Prostitution, 9
Psychosis, 9
Psychotropic drugs, 132
Public transportation for disabled, 137, 159
Purgatives, 3

Quayle, Vice President Dan, 147
Quilt auction for Sunshine Children's Home, 102
Quota Club of Toledo, 32

Racism and physical characteristics, 62
Radcliffe College, 23
Randolph-Shepard Act, 158
Reagan, President Ronald, 135
Receiving hospital, 11
Reconstructing the Crippled Soldier, 45
Red Cross, 27, 45
Red Cross Institute for Crippled and Disabled Men, 45
Reeve, Christopher, 153
Regional Disability History Archive Project, iv, v, vii
Rehabilitation Act of 1973, 133, 159
Rehabilitation Act of 1978, 160
Religious excitement, 9
Retarded, x, 151
Richards, Susan, 79
Richey, John, 27
Ridge School, Bowling Green, Ohio, 100, 106-107
Ripley, S. Dillon, 133
Roberts, Ed, 134-136
Roberts, Emma, 48
Roeger, Shirley, 115, 117-119
Rogers, Roy, 96
Rolling Quads, 135
Roosevelt Memorial, Washington, D.C., 82, 82, 91
Roosevelt, Eleanor, 79
Roosevelt, Franklin Delano, 28, 51, 157, 161
Roosevelt, Franklin Delano and polio, 77-79, 82, 84
Roosevelt, Theodore, 77
Rosewood Presbyterian Church, Toledo, 99
Rotary Club of Toledo—See Toledo Rotary Club
Rotary International, 50, 55
Rotary of Elyria—See Elyria Rotary
Rotary of Ohio—See Ohio Rotary
Ryan White C.A.R.E. Act, 152, 161

Sabin, Albert, 80
Salk vaccine, 82
Salk, Jonas, 70
Salvation Army, 119
Sanger, Margaret, 62
Saxton, Frank, 26
Schmidt, Carl, 107
Schools for the blind, 24
Scott High School, 29
Section 504, Rehabilitation Act of 1973, 133-134, 159-160
Seduction, 9
Seguin, Edouard, 95
Sentinel Tribune, Bowling Green, 30
Sexton, Tommy, 123
Sexual self abuse, 9
Sheltered Workshop Foundation of Lucas County, Inc., 105
Sheltered workshops for blind, 158
Shepard, George, 81
Shriver, Eunice Kennedy, 97
Shuer, Jay, 110
Sight Center Audio Network, 30
Sight Center of Northwest Ohio, 29-30
Silent Club—See Toledo Silent Club,
Small Business Administration and employment of disabled, 124
Smith, Hoke, 115
Smith-Sears Veterans Rehabilitation Act of 1918, 157
Smithsonian Institution, 133
Social Darwinism, 62
Social Security Act of 1935, 115, 158
Social Security Amendments of 1950, 158
Social Security Amendments of 1972, 159
Social Security Amendments of 1980, 160
Social Security Disability Insurance, 117, 158
Social Security Disability Reform Act, 160
Social Services Federation, 16

Sommerset Court, England, 103
Special Olympics, 97
Spencer, Herbert, 62
Squire, Sam, 49
St. Andrew's Episcopal Church, 100
St. Anthony's Villa, 82
St. Vincent dePaul, 119
Standart, Will, 50, 58
Standart-Simmons Hardware Store, 50
Statistics on disabled in Lucas County, 117
Statistics on employment of disabled, 117
Sterilization of developmentally disabled, 96
Sterilization of disabled, 62, 64, 157
Sullivan, Anne, 23
Sullivan, Joe F., 45-48
Sunshine Children's Home, 101-103, 109
Super Race, 65
Supplemental Security Income, 159
Surgical implants for the deaf, 153
Swan Creek, 8
Swayne, Noah, 25, 27
Switzer, Mary, 133
Syphillis, 9-10

T4, 66-67
TDD, 32
Technology-Related Assistance Act for Individuals with Disabilities, 160
Telecommunications for the Disabled Act, 160
Tiergartenstrasse No. 4, 66
Tobey, H.A., 3, 8-10, 14-15
Toledo Ad Club, 65
Toledo and polio epidemic of 1935, 75
Toledo Area Regional Transit Authority, 137
Toledo Board of Education, 50, 81, 99
Toledo Chamber of Commerce, 26, 99
Toledo Community Chest, 25-27
Toledo Contagious Disease Hospital, 75

Toledo Deaf Club, 32
Toledo Federation of Charities, 54
Toledo Health Department, 80
Toledo Lions Club, 25-27, 29
Toledo Mental Health Center, 11
Toledo Public Schools, 103
Toledo Rotary Club, 32, 43, 46-48, 50-51, 55, 58, 80-81, 119
Toledo School for the Deaf and Hard of Hearing, 32, 37
Toledo Silent Club, 32
Toledo Society for Crippled Children, 49, 80-82, 136
Toledo Society for the Blind, 26-29, 37-39
Toledo Society for the Handicapped, 136-137, 143-145
Toledo State Asylum for the Insane, 9, 15, 17
Toledo State Hospital, 3, 7-11, 14-16, 18-20, 65
To-St-Ho newspaper, 10
Toward Independence: An Assessment of Federal Laws and Programs Affecting Persons with Disabilities, 136, 160
Tracy School, 99
Transmission of HIV/AIDS, 153
Truman, President Harry S, 158
Twain, Mark, 24

U.S. Department of Health, Education, and Welfare, 116, 120, 124, 160
U.S. Department of Housing and Urban Development, 152
Unheard Cry, 45
United States v. Karl Brandt, 68
United Way, 25
University of California at Berkeley, 134, 135
University of Toledo, 79
University of Toledo and disabled students, 119, 131, 137-140

University of Toledo College of Arts and Sciences, 65
Urban Mass Transit Act, 159

Valentine Building, 26
Van Leuvan Browne Hospital, Detroit, 47
Veterans with disabilities, 44
Village idiots, 95
Virginia and sterilization of disabled, 157, 159, 161
Vocational rehabilitation, 114-127, 131, 158
Vocational Rehabilitation Amendments of 1965, 159
Vocational training for developmental disabilities, 96, 98-99
Volunteers of America, 119
Voting Accessibility for the Elderly and Handicapped Act, 160
W. N. Gates Hospital for Sick, Crippled, and Deformed Children, 49, 53

Walker, John, 132
Ward M. Canaday Center for Special Collections, iv, vi, x
Warm Springs, Georgia, 51, 77-79, 86, 123
Warm Springs: Traces of a Childhood at FDR's Polio Haven, 79
Warren, Supreme Court Justice Earl, 133
Washington sterilization law, 64
Wheelchair Review, 79
Whitaker, Thomas, 27, 36
White House Conference on Handicapped Individuals, 129-130, 126-127
White, Ryan, 152
Willowbrook State School, Long Island, New York, 97
Wills, Harry, 26

Wilson, President Woodrow, 115
Women's Hospital, Toledo State Hospital, 16
Wood County Association for Retarded Children, 107
Wood County Board of Mental Retardation and Developmental Disabilities, 100, 106, 111
Wood Lane Industries, 100
Wood Lane School, 100, 111
Workers' compensation, 157
Works Progress Administration and employment of disabled, 158
World Institute on Disability, 135
World War I, 10, 45, 115
World War I and disability, 45
World War II, 10, 115-116
Wright, A.B., 6-7
Wright, Nackie, 50, 56
WSPD Radio, 79

Zeigler Rehabilitation Homes, 103
Zeigler, Charlotte, 103